THE PORCH SERIES

THE PORCH SERIES

SELF-DISCOVERY, GROWTH,

& HEALING IN THE SHADOW

OF SEX ADDICTION

CAT CLARK
A Survivor of Partner Betrayal

SANO PRESS, LLC
CLAREMONT, CA

SANO PRESS, LLC
CLAREMONT, CA

Copyright © 2023 by Cat Clark. All rights reserved. No part of this publication may be used or reproduced, stored or entered into a retrieval system, transmitted, photocopied, recorded, or otherwise reproduced in any form by any mechanical or electronic means, without the prior written permission of the authors and Sano Press, with the exception of brief quotations for the purposes of review articles.

1st Edition

Layout, book design, graphic design by Chris Bordey. Mountain heart cover designed by Chris Bordey with the assistance of AI. Fonts in use through Open Font License or through system fonts.

Sano Press feather trademark Sano Press, LLC.

ISBN-13: 978-1-956620-03-0

Disclaimer

The information provided in this book is for educational purposes only and should not be considered a substitute for professional medical or health advice. It is not intended to replace professional diagnosis, treatment, or guidance. The content is based on general knowledge, the author's personal experiences, and the author's research, but may not be applicable to individual circumstances. The author and publisher are not liable for any actions taken based on the information presented. Consult a qualified healthcare professional for personalized medical advice and treatment.

Dedication

~

I'd like to dedicate my story to the partners of sexual addiction. This is the first book I've ever written and I know it will trigger a lot of emotions for me and those who peruse it. Being married to or in a relationship with a sexual addict is a very painful experience. I believe it's an "invisible silent killer" and the worst addiction.

I'm a Christian and believe in God. Without His guidance and support, I would not be able to call myself a "Victor" instead of a "Victim." I'm deeply grateful for this opportunity to share my story and hope I serve my readers well. If I am able to help just one person, my time will be well spent.

From the bottom of my heart, I thank the Founding Director, Dr. Michael Barta (PH.D., LPC, CSAT-S) and the Clinical Director and Partner Specialist Juliane Rohs (MMA, MFT, LCSW) at "Begin Again Institute" in Boulder, Colorado. Dr. Barta has thirty-one years' experience and Juliane has twenty-three years' experience in the field of sexual addiction. I have named them "The Dynamic Duo." They are very caring, thorough, and comfortable to be around. The knowledge I received was priceless. Going to "Begin Again" was the best decision we've ever made.

I strongly urge you to seek professional counseling with a sexual addiction specialist who can explain how this ugly addiction can manifest itself into your loved one. Pornography is readily available through social media, the internet, and even commercials. Sexual addiction is a *respecter of none—at the time of writing this, I was sixty-seven years old and my husband was sixty-five. Who'd have thought Grandpa and Grandma would have dealt with something this damaging? We worked very hard to save our marriage and destroy the evil addict that was trying to steal our right to have the life God intended.*

To my sons, Jeff and Mark, I'm so grateful God chose me to be your mother. You've grown up to be wonderful men, and I'm so proud of you! Your love and support have carried me through some very rough times.

The day will come when I leave to be with my heavenly Father and you won't physically see me. But I promise, I'll always be watching over you.

Love, Mom

"I can do all things through Christ who gives me strength."

TABLE of CONTENTS

FOREWORD TO THE PORCH SERIES..................12-14

PART I: GET OFF MY PORCH—UNVEILING THE SHADOWS OF ADDICTION 15-90

1. Our Love/Hate Relationship..17
2. The First Separation.. 24
3. Cat's Health Crisis 28
4. Frank's Intensive Counseling 35
5. Cat's Intensive Counseling.. 40
6. The Peaceful Separation 50
7. A Letter to the Addiction... 57
8. Frank's Destructive Behavior...................................... 60
9. My Recovery Plan 76
10. Restoring Intimacy 80
11. Summary... 87
12. A Letter to My Love 90

PART II: SITTING ON THE PORCH SWING—NAVIGATING THE DEPTHS OF SEPARATION & PTSD **91-140**

13. Our New Beginning 93

14. Cat's in the Cradle 95

15. Separation Preparation 99

16. Proverbs 32 107

17. Cat's Ball of Yarn 112

18. Shame and Blame 117

19. Emotional Roller-Coaster 122

20. Waiting to Pounce 127

21. Cat's PTSD Recovery Plan 133

22. Summary 137

23. Someday 140

PART III: SWEEPING THE PORCH—ENFORCING BOUNDARIES & RECLAIMING MY INDEPENDENCE **141-188**

24. Shut the Door 143

25. My Powerful Broom 145

26. Identifying Limits 147

27. The Chains that Bind 151

28. The Other Family 156

29. Toxic Family Members 160

30. Fear of Setting Boundaries 166

31. The "S" Word 171

32. Don't Drink the Poison 178

33. Take Control of Your Sanity 181

34. Summary 186

PART IV: MY PORCH LIGHT—EMBRACING A NEW CHAPTER & THE ROAD TO RECOVERY 189-249

35. Be Still and Know 191

36. The Light 195

37. The Fallen Princess 199

38. The Unwelcomed Guest 203

39. Time to Get Real 210

40. D-Day 217

41. Take It Slow—Let It Go 223

42. A Year Ago Today 226

43. Lessons Learned 231

44. I Will Survive 243

45. Dear God 247

ABOUT THE AUTHOR 251

Foreword to The Porch Series

The *Porch Series* is a compilation of four separate books I authored that were individually published while I was going through the horrific emotional pain I suffered from being married to a sex addict for nineteen years. With the help of professional counseling and extensive research, I chose to educate myself about the addiction and betrayal trauma that a partner suffers. I was able to apply the knowledge I received, which helped tremendously with my own recovery.

These books tell my personal story of moving from "victim" to "victor" and how I overcame the pain using valuable recovery techniques I discovered and share with my readers. These books also contain the heartbreak and many struggles we had as a couple that you most likely can relate to. I pray that this book helps you realize that you are not alone and with the help of God, you can heal and move forward to a healthy and fulfilling life.

Now that I'm a real live author, I've discovered one of the biggest challenges is to choose an appropriate title for your book, and I can't continue without telling you how the titles for *The Porch Series* were chosen. These were originally written as four separate books, and they were combined into one to create *The Porch Series*.

To start with the first book, *Get Off My Porch*, I was talking with two dearly beloved friends, and one of them suggested I should write a book about my experience with a sexual addict. That caught me off guard, but I thought about it and decided I might give it a shot. We came up with several ideas for a title, but nothing seemed to click. Out of the blue, one of them quietly said *Get Off My Porch*, and we all immediately agreed. I told him that was an awesome title, and he pointed up and said, "It didn't come from me." I have to admit, I got goosebumps. That one statement told me that I had been chosen by God to tackle this project, so here I am. I'm proud to serve him.

Next, I figured out that I needed to write a sequel about Frank and I going through our recovery. I thought I was done writing, but God evidently had other plans for me. I'll never understand why He puts ideas in my head while I'm in the shower and don't have anything to write on, but *Sitting on the Porch Swing* also popped up for the second book.

When I thought more about the title, I realized that's how people become acquainted and get to know each other—just leisurely hanging out. Since I have never met the *real* Frank because he came to me as an addict (which we didn't know until he was diagnosed) this could get interesting. In the past, I never let a man into my home until I got to know him well. Since we are still married, I can't let Frank move back in until I know he can be trusted and has the addict under control. I have the right as his wife to feel safe and loved as God commands, and I'll settle for nothing less.

Then, while doing my research for *The Porch Series*, I discovered I needed to start setting boundaries around a few people who I allowed to control me. I educated myself, applied that knowledge, and am eager to share it with my readers. *Sweeping the Porch* provides vital information on how to effectively set boundaries. I encourage you to get your powerful broom out and clear the path to your mind where all the hurtful and negative thoughts dwell. When you allow others to control you, it can steal your peace, joy, and self-esteem. Sweep out all the ugly, replace it with positive thinking, and dream about a future of peace and security. Be vigilant, be strong, and exercise your right to control your life!

Finally, I picked the title *My Porch Light* for my last book of the series for a reason. When someone knocks on your door at night, your immediate reaction is to turn on the porch light to see who's there. If it's someone you know and trust you'll let them in, and if not, you'll close the door and lock it. The same is applicable to people who are toxic in your life. Shut the door because it's all about safety.

—Cat Clark

PART I

GET OFF MY PORCH:

UNVEILING THE SHADOWS OF ADDICTION

Chapter 1

OUR LOVE/HATE RELATIONSHIP

On September 9, 2017 my fears became a reality. I was taking my husband Frank to the airport for a two-week intensive program for sexual addiction. As I pulled away from the baggage check-in, the sadness and anger were overwhelming. The man of my dreams who I thought would love and cherish me forever had become the enemy.

My name is Cat. I am sixty-seven years old, and my husband Frank is sixty-five. We've been married for nineteen years, and this is the second marriage for both of us. On our wedding day, I truly believed it was going to be "till death do us part." I must have interpreted those words differently because when I learned of his addiction, I thought I was going to die, and now we have indeed parted.

I don't like the word "hate" and thought I knew how it felt, but his sexual addiction triggered an emotion in me I didn't realize existed—hatred. I know it's a sin to hate, but I have to admit I have experienced that emotion during this marriage. It's horrible.

When we met, I was a personal trainer in a local health club, and Frank was a member. I had left my previous husband and had set up a house for myself. Frank had been divorced for two years. A mutual friend, who just happened to be his ex-girlfriend, introduced us. She told me he was a good man but not her type. He and I hit it off and became friends quickly.

When we started dating, he invited me to church. Our higher power is God, and I was excited that he attended church regularly. I discovered he knew the Bible very well, which became the topic of many discussions.

I have two sons who are the loves of my life. When we started dating, the oldest one was twenty-four and lived in Colorado.

PART I: GET OFF MY PORCH

The youngest was nineteen and in the Marines. They met Frank during their visits home. They seemed a bit cautious but didn't disrespect him. To this day, my sons totally accept, respect, and love him, and he loves them like his own children.

About a year and a half into dating, Frank surprised me and proposed to me in church. Of course, I accepted. It was a beautiful moment. He had the proposal audio taped, and we decided we would play it on every anniversary. Six months later, we had a beautiful wedding and began our new life. I moved into his home a week before the wedding and looked forward to my wonderful, glorious life with Mr. Frank.

I think at this point I need to give you a short background on our families. Frank was basically an only child. His sister was eleven years older and left home at a young age. His parents both worked, so he didn't receive much of their time. His grandparents also lived with them, so Grandma was in charge most of the time. His social life consisted of friends outside of the home. He didn't have much of a father figure and learned that he had to make his own way in life.

I was number four of five siblings. Our home was very active, and there was no question that we were loved. We respected our parents, who encouraged us to pursue any interests, and we were well supported in everything we chose to do. We played table games that our parents participated in and were free to talk about any problems we had. I have no complaints about my childhood—I was very fortunate.

Three months into the marriage, his interest in being intimate with me faded. I was so hurt and confused because I thought I'd done something to cause it. I confronted him about it, and he basically told me that I had an insecurity problem and was imagining it.

The computer was downstairs, and he'd check his email almost daily which would take a lot of time because he said most of it was work related. I learned early in the marriage not to disturb him during those times because he'd "lose his train of thought."

Back when we first started dating, Frank went on a business trip, asked me to tend to his cat, and gave me a key to the house. He had already tried to find out if I was interested in pornography, and after I let him know I wasn't, he assured me he felt the same way. While he was gone, I got curious and checked his computer, and I found pornography as well as some inappropriate video tapes.

Of course, we had a heated discussion when he got back from his trip, and he assured me that he was done with it and would get rid of everything. His excuse for even having that type of trash was because most single men do it, but now that he had me there was no reason to keep it. Since he was a Christian, I believed him. Looking back, that was not Christian behavior.

After we were married, curiosity got the better of me one day after he left for work, and I checked the computer. But, I found nothing. I wasn't computer savvy at the time, so I didn't even think about checking the history and honestly didn't know how. For the next few months, he continued to ignore me in the bedroom, so I started getting suspicious again and asked a friend how to check the history. Well, I just about had a heart attack when I pulled it up. The filthy images were everywhere, and I thought I was going to be physically sick.

I confronted him, and he assured me that those were only pop-ups and that he deleted them immediately when that happened. Not being educated on pop-ups either, I once again believed him. I feel pretty stupid now, knowing that a deleted page won't show up in the history (I'm now educated on the computer).

He started to pay more attention to me in the bedroom, but it didn't last. I continued to check the computer, but he was always one step ahead of me and deleted all the inappropriate sites he'd been to. I began to take his neglect in the bedroom very personally. I became ashamed of my body, which I initially thought was pretty good for age forty-eight, but I could never measure up to those young perfect bodies I'd seen on the computer. The most credit I gave myself was that I had a pretty face, green eyes, and good hair.

To compensate for what I saw as inadequacies in myself, I became "Little Miss Do-Gooder." I've always kept a good house but became obsessive with cleaning, cooking, crafts, yard work, etc. I did everything I could to get his attention and show him I was worthy, but nothing in the bedroom changed. He occasionally wanted me (or so I thought), but I now realize it wasn't me he was with. Looking back, I should have divorced him, but I was determined to make the marriage work because I loved everything else about him as a husband. He's a good man in so many ways except for the most important in a marriage—intimacy inside and outside of the bedroom.

Frank noticed the change in me, but instead of standing up and doing what was right, he convinced me that I was the problem and insisted I go to counseling with our pastor—which I did. After listening to my sad story, our pastor's advice was: "Just love him the way God commands." Excuse me, but this man was far from loveable!

I discovered many years later through one of the local counselors (not the final intensive treatment) that he had a problem with pornography. His sexual preferences were disgusting and repulsive images on the TV and computer. I still worked at the health club and watched him objectify women, and he occasionally used my body to fulfill his fantasies. My life was less than happy, but I allowed him to mistreat me because I still had hope—I wasn't going to give up on the "for better or worse" part of our marriage vows.

I soon learned it wasn't safe for me to go anywhere with him because he didn't care that I was standing right there—he still stared at and studied younger women. He wanted what he wanted, and if he hurt me to get it, too bad. If I confronted him,

I was told it was my imagination and that I was insecure. He actually made me believe I was the problem. However, he became more careful about hiding his bad behavior and paid more attention to me.

When we first started dating, the ex-girlfriend who had introduced us started calling Frank on a regular basis when he was at my house. Whatever she needed, he would immediately leave and attend to her needs. They both assured me they had stayed friends and since she was a single mother, she needed a man to help out occasionally. This became a huge problem for me when she began calling for trivial stuff, and I told him it was over. He severed the relationship with her, and we patched things up.

He had a daughter in college who didn't live at home, but she would go to church with us twice a month when she visited him. I should have known from the beginning there was a problem when I was placed in the backseat of the car. I was ignored on the ride and opened the door to let myself out. It didn't take long to discover that he allowed his daughter to control him. Being an optimist, I assumed things would change in time because it was an adjustment for everyone. Unfortunately, they got much worse. Looking back, there were many signs that I missed about the relationship with his daughter, but I was in love with him and didn't want to rock the boat.

Her visits became explosive after we were married. I had "rules" that she set and was expected to obey them. Most of my clothes hung in the basement even though there was an empty closet in her childhood bedroom. She complained about the food I had prepared, the temperature in the house, and where the furniture I brought into the marriage was placed, and she had a host of ridiculous demands. I had no control over anything while she was there. She invited her mother over when she wished, and I was expected to comply. He did nothing—even after I threatened to leave.

PART I: GET OFF MY PORCH

While we were on our honeymoon, his ex-wife used the spare key in the garage, which he forgot to remove, and came into our marital home. She stole a box of leather coats and some of my boots and hats, and she invaded my intimate apparel drawer, which she left in disarray. Frank did nothing about that either. At that point, I realized his ex-wife also controlled him.

Before we married, we agreed that we would look for another house to buy if I wasn't comfortable in his home. I was certainly ready to do just that. We found one, and I was elated. However, up jumped the Devil again! The daughter continued to take control, and the ex-wife was once again coming into our new home. Well, the new bride was done being cooperative, and the fight was on. I won't bore you with the details, but I won and no one was physically hurt. My spineless husband did not help, so I handled it myself. Mr. Frank quickly respected the boundaries I put on her.

After we had been married about six months and the daughter was planning her wedding, I assumed things would change once she had her own home. In the meantime, she graduated from college. When it was time for family pictures, I was told to sit on the bleachers, and his ex-wife's husband was invited to join them. You got it—Mr. Frank hung his head and went up there like a trained dog. I assumed his daughter was angry about the boundaries I set on her mother, so I sat there like the good little step-momma. I still desperately tried to fit into the chaos.

Then it was time for his daughter to get married. We went to the wedding rehearsal, and I was told I would have to sit in the back row of the church while her dad would walk her down the aisle and sit in front. He told her he didn't think it was right. Of course, she won. I lost my dad before we were married and have an awesome step-dad who informed me he would walk me down the aisle to sit with my husband, and that's just what we did. It was kind of a fun moment because she didn't expect it.

Bad start, right? The signs were all over, and yet I still believed in time things would change because he loved me. It didn't take long to figure out that my new husband was a coward and had no respect for me.

During the next ten years, the relationship went up and down, and the addict became more aggressive. Frank was getting a bit too big for his britches. His need to control and manipulate caused many arguments and dissension in the marriage. I caught him lying so much and finally realized it was habitual. The "love/hate" relationship had begun. He would push me until I reached the boiling point then become loving and attentive for a short time. Arguments became the norm, and we started drifting apart. That's when my trust in him died.

I was a mess and knew something had to be done. I couldn't live like this anymore.

PART I: GET OFF MY PORCH

Chapter 2

THE FIRST SEPARATION

Frank's daughter was now married and had two children. She was still controlling. I confronted Frank about how her behavior affected our marriage, but he continuously made excuses for her. I'm ashamed to admit that I still allowed her to control me to avoid conflict. I never asked him to choose between me and his daughter. He loves her, and I have no right to interfere with that love. I was simply asking him to demand the respect we were entitled to.

Early in the marriage, I developed chronic insomnia and ended up with depression. I was now retired, but Frank still worked. I absolutely detested my body and started wearing black when he was around because I felt like my body disgusted him. I knew he was still acting out, but I couldn't catch him and didn't have any proof. He continued to objectify women and rarely asked me to be with him intimately. Looking back to when he asked me to marry him, I believe I had all the qualities he was looking for in a wife with the exception of my body. It was almost as if he was hiring an employee. I was the good little wife who did her domestic jobs but felt unloved and alone.

Then, it happened. He was working an evening shift and sleeping in the bedroom downstairs. I was asleep, but suddenly my eyes popped open because I knew something was wrong. I walked into the kitchen and heard sounds coming from downstairs, and it was quite obvious what he was doing. I went back to bed and cried myself to sleep, but I confronted him the next day. That was a huge breaking point for me—I told him he had to leave. After he left, a wonderful peace set in, and I felt safe. I realized that my internal light dimmed when he was around.

I began to think about how he had treated me and realized that I had been lied to, manipulated, controlled, disrespected, and emotionally abandoned. My energy level had slowed down, and my body physically hurt. I had always been healthy and worked out on a regular basis, but depression held me down. I believe if he would have been standing before me, I would have used all the strength I had to beat him senseless. I became angry and decided he was not worthy of my love.

He had moved in with an elder from the church. The day after he left, I went to a lawyer with the intent of divorcing him. We started talking on the phone, and it became pretty obvious that he assumed it would be a short stay. I told him he needed counseling for his emotional abuse and for acting out towards me. He went to a Christian counselor, got his book and workbook, and seemed to be making progress. We were separated for seven months. I had made the decision to file for a divorce, so I invited him over to peruse the papers. At that point he broke down, fell to his knees, and asked for another chance. I felt such pity for him that I gave in. As far as the counseling, I found out years later that he was telling the counselor only what he thought she wanted to hear and was not actively working the program.

He eventually confronted his daughter and was punished with the loss of his grandchildren for almost two years. They have since reconciled, and he is allowed to see the grandkids a couple times a month. I have no idea what his relationship is with her, but I have severed all ties, although I continue to pray for her.

After he moved back in, he said we needed to make some changes to help him recover and make me feel safe. He took off his glasses when we were out in public so he could prove to me that he was not objectifying women. He started changing stations on the TV if an inappropriate commercial came on. He asked me to put parental locks on ratings. He started paying attention to me—even in the bedroom.

PART I: GET OFF MY PORCH

We seemed to be getting closer, and I started to trust him a little at a time. But just when I would get comfortable, he would destroy my progress by acting out, lying, manipulating, or controlling. He also instructed me to not approach him about intimacy because he would feel pressured to perform. Any affection I felt for him was gone.

About three years ago, I decided to stay with him and hope for the best because I had developed serious health issues due to the emotional abuse and needed the insurance. I didn't want him sexually, and the thought of being with him repulsed me. But oddly enough, I still loved him and hoped he would change.

I believe this is a good place to insert a letter I sent to Frank while he was out of state for treatment last year. It explains how I felt for over eighteen years but previously couldn't put into words.

> *God has created me as a human. I am made to age, die, and hopefully make it to Heaven. But to some men, a woman is not given the luxury to age and still be attractive and desirable. We are replaced with fantasy women, pornography, or adultery, but we are expected to feel loved.*
>
> *It's not my fault that I don't look twenty-years-old anymore—nor do you. In the mind of an addict, an aging woman is like an old car that needs to be replaced. Men want a newer model but keep the old car in a garage locked from the outside. They may drive it occasionally, but it's not nearly as pretty as the newer model. That's the best way I can describe how I feel, but I have been replaced with your fantasy of younger women. You take care of yourself but not me.*
>
> *My skin is not firm and my shape is not perfect, but I still have a heart and good morals. I'm able to get around pretty well and look younger than I am. I should be able to feel good about that, but my*

*husband's behavior keeps me feeling unloved
and unwanted.*

*I feel that your neglect and behavior disrespects
God's plan for me. You must truly feel that I'm
desirable and attractive because you passed those
questions on the polygraph, but your behavior does
not match your answers.*

*At this point in my life I should feel safe and secure,
but I don't. I think the combination of everything
I've written here is the cause of the sadness I told
you about. I've worked very hard my entire adult
life to be healthy and look good, but it seems like
you don't appreciate it. I don't think I've ever felt as
lonely as I do now. If God wasn't in my life, I don't
know what I'd do!*

*Why do men think that no matter how old they are
and no matter how they look that they have the
right to judge and compare their aging wives to a
younger woman? You act as though I don't have the
right to age but you do. Maybe it's time for you to
get your Bible out and see what God says about how
a man is supposed to love his wife.*

After he moved back in, we jumped from counselor to counselor in an attempt to save the marriage, but nothing worked. At the time, we didn't realize that he was a sexual addict. He became angry with himself because he realized that I had shut down and became distant. His frustration triggered his need to control and manipulate me again to "get me back in line," but I just didn't care anymore.

PART I: GET OFF MY PORCH

Chapter 3

CAT'S HEALTH CRISIS

I had no idea that depression could cause severe health problems, but I sure found out the hard way! I experienced sadness, rejection, and depression in the early days of the marriage. I thought for sure I was going to die of a broken heart. I started self-talks to get my emotions back on track and thought I was handling things rather well because I've always been able to rationally deal with adverse situations. Over time, I allowed his behavior to change who I was, and my health suffered severely. I compare it to the story of the boiling frog. If you put a frog on the stove in a pot of cold water and gradually turn up the heat until it begins to boil, the frog doesn't jump out—it acclimates to the temperature and dies (but trust me, I've never murdered a frog). That's exactly what happened to me. The addict was slowly destroying me.

Having experienced the manipulation and control of an addict for nineteen years, I now realize how they gain control. Addicts use gaslighting, which means they purposely confuse you and make you believe it's your fault in order to manipulate and gain control. It can truly make you feel like you're going crazy. Through manipulation, lies, and victim mentality behavior, they make you believe you're the problem because of insecurity. They can also make you believe you're imagining their inappropriate behaviors because you don't feel good about yourself. They put on their sad face of rejection and pout because you don't trust them, even though they're good people and love you oh-so-very-much. Over time, they can convince you that they are the victim. There will come a time when you actually feel sorry for them. You'll feel guilty because you've accused them of treating you poorly. That's when you enter the danger zone and the self-persecution starts.

But once your fears become a reality, the relationship takes a deadly turn. You know without a doubt you're involved with a pervert, sex addict, or whatever title you chose to give them. The addict becomes relaxed because they assume they have you "in line." They believe you won't approach them about their behavior because you feel guilty about how you treated them in the past. They become bold but careless and don't take as many precautions to hide their sin. If you do confront them, the fight is on and *you will not win*. They will stay in the game until they beat you down emotionally, and you'll more than likely give up to end the fight. However, your stress level jumps up another notch with each confrontation, and it can eventually affect your health and emotional state. Just remember, an addict will not hesitate to lie when cornered. Over time, they start lying about insignificant things, and that's when the trust in all areas of the marriage dies.

I'm embarrassed to admit that I fell into the ugly pit of self-persecution. I loathed my body so much that I actually clawed at my stomach and left scratches because it had gotten bigger due to Prednisone. I have pulled out handfuls of my hair because I was so frustrated. Of course, I ended up with a whopper of a headache each time, but it didn't matter. I've actually stared at myself in the mirror and verbally cussed myself out for being so disgusting. I have no idea how many panic attacks I've suffered over the years. They became so frequent that I applied my yoga knowledge and handled them with breathing techniques. I prayed and cried until I became physically and emotionally exhausted.

When I shopped for clothes, I cried in the fitting room when something didn't fit right and decided I didn't deserve anything. I was a size 14 and sometimes 16 due to my protruding stomach. I went to a plastic surgeon to inquire about liposuction, and he said I didn't have enough fat to qualify for the procedure. I was devastated. I thought that if I looked better he'd want me. But I found out later that it wouldn't have mattered—I wasn't the problem, the addiction was.

I was so depressed and insecure that I gave up piano lessons. I've taken them for a long time and was in the last book of the series, but I decided I wasn't any good. During the last recital last November, I froze during rehearsal and never went back. During my counseling session, I discovered it was because Frank was in the room and in my mind he was judging me. The addict will kill your spirit if you allow him to.

I believe it's important for you to know the health risks involved if you allow the addict to get total control. Frank's sexual addiction took me down physically and emotionally. I thought he was the light at the end of the tunnel, but unfortunately he was a train coming right at me!

My immune system started going down fast, and I was in serious trouble. I couldn't sleep, hurt everywhere, and broke out with a painful rash (many times) that covered about every area of my body. My face looked like a burn victim, and I avoided leaving the house. Sometimes the pain brought me to tears—I thought I was going to lose my mind and feared I was going to die.

My oldest son lives in Colorado and is pretty educated in natural herbs. He convinced me to come out and be examined by his kinesiologist. The doctor did muscle testing and prescribed pure, natural herbs for my immune system, thyroid, iron, and all the deficiencies my body had suffered. I had to drink the herbs, which tasted like the smell of a dead animal, but my health substantially improved after I stayed on the program for two years. Since then, I've been on whole food supplements and am very dedicated. I know if I don't keep my body healthy, I'll get sick again.

Over the course of several years I ended up taking ten rounds of Prednisone, which caused weight gain and is not good for someone who already hates their body. I went to several specialists before I was diagnosed with an allergic reaction to preservatives in personal products and household cleaners. My immune system couldn't fight for me. I've been told by several doctors that this is a life sentence, and I will always have to be proactive. It is also a condition that is induced by stress. So, I had to control my stress level while living with a sex addict—very difficult.

Several years ago, I also learned the hard way that inhalation of certain chemicals can lead to anaphylactic shock, which, of course, can kill you. We had a contractor painting the inside of our home, and my skin started burning. I broke out in a rash that set me on fire. I left the premises and went to a relative's house to apply my topical medication. I got a severe migraine, and two days later, my throat started closing. I ended up in the ER and was hospitalized for several days.

My second episode occurred when I was on vacation in Nevada with my cousin. I wasn't exposed to any chemicals, but once again, I was rushed to the ER just in time. I remembered that I was upset because I saw couples who appeared to be happy and also perverts who were hitting on women. The realization of how damaged and pitiful my life was sent my stress level over the top. I asked the doctor if I was in trouble, and he said yes. I knew I was headed for anaphylactic shock, but I got there just in time.

While Frank was out-of-state for his intensive program and before I went for my partner counseling, I asked the facility about reading material for myself so I could have a better understanding of sexual addiction. They recommended *Your Sexually Addicted Spouse* by Barbara Steffens, plus a workbook called *Facing Heartbreak* by Stefanie Carnes. I absolutely would recommend both of these books to any partner dealing with a sexual addict. They are tough reads, but the knowledge you gain will be worth it.

While reading the book, I was totally shocked when I discovered I had 24 out of the 27 signs and symptoms of post-traumatic stress disorder (PTSD). There are two types of trauma in PTSD: physiological and psychological. I was diagnosed with psychological trauma during my treatment. This is my list of symptoms:

- Hyperarousal
- Reliving the event
- Helplessness
- Hyper-vigilance
- Sleeplessness
- Anxiety
- Nightmares
- Intrusive images
- Panic attacks
- Oversensitivity
- Dissociation
- Health problems
- Withdrawing
- Phobias
- Depression

- Inability to eat
- Chronic fatigue
- Avoidance
- Restlessness
- Flashbacks
- Immune/Endocrine system deficiency
- Mood swings
- Confusion
- Rage

There's no way I can describe my reaction without cussing like a sailor, but I will say the last one on my list, rage, pretty much covers it. The only symptoms I lacked were immobility, overeating, and denial. I knew I had to be totally honest when I checked my symptoms if I was going to recover. I'll admit that I went over the list two more times hoping to find something that I accidentally checked but found nothing.

I was sitting on the patio listening to the birds sing in what I call "my little Garden of Eden" when I read this section. I cried a bit, then gently slammed the book into the fence. My dog does not fetch, but she raced over to see what the commotion was all about. I guess you already figured out that I was being facetious when I said "gently slammed the book." The fence was probably about twenty feet away from the patio. To say I was upset is an understatement—I was absolutely livid! Realizing that the filthy addict who resided in my husband's mind was to blame for my illness took me to a different place.

So, I put on my big girl panties and decided that I'd had enough. This addict was not going to take me down. I made the decision that day to beat PTSD and become a victor instead of a victim. At first I had a vision in my head of sitting in a crowded room with other women and saying: "Hello, I'm Cat, and I'm the victim of a sexual addict." No way! Not gonna happen! I'd always stood up for myself and could do it again. The addict had me face down with his foot on my back, but now I would stand up and fight this invisible demon. He'd taken all he was going to from me. With God on my side, I would prevail!

Today, as I continue to write my book, my health has improved substantially, but I still have to be on guard wherever I go. I intend to beat this "life sentence" and will never stop fighting until I prove the doctors wrong. With God all things are possible.

Please guard your heart and your body. The addict is cruel and will stop at nothing to have their way. You will be the one who has to do damage control because of someone else's addiction. Let me be an example of what the consequences could be if you fall into that abyss. Know that you're a child of God and He did not create you to be abused.

Chapter 4

FRANK'S INTENSIVE COUNSELING

Nine years had passed since Frank returned from the first separation, and we were approaching our nineteenth wedding anniversary. Of course, he was on his best behavior for a few months after he moved back, but it didn't last. I had learned to adjust to an unfulfilling, miserable life. I resented his mere presence. We got along okay, but I was too tired and depressed to even care. The depression got worse, and a good night's sleep was rare. He was still working, so I treasured my time alone during the day. I could relax and be myself. I felt safe because he wasn't here. But when it was time for him to come home, I knew my feeling of safety would be gone.

Boring doesn't begin to describe the life we shared. The highlight of the week was going to stock up at Walmart on Saturday. Of course, it was torture for me because he felt that it was his job to check out younger women and ignore me. Over time, I trained myself to not look at his face while we were out in public to avoid the pain it caused. Watching television was not a leisure experience because he would become fixated with the images of younger women. Occasionally we would go out to eat, but then there were waitresses to deal with.

There are younger and prettier women everywhere, and a new crop appears every year. I knew I would never measure up to his fantasy girls. He rarely approached me for sex, and when he did, I complied like the good wife to keep the peace. It was demeaning and degrading because I knew I was being used. I'd never felt so unloved in my life.

My hurt and anger eventually turned into rage. His last indiscretion was the last straw for me. I knew something was very wrong with him. I told him to either get help or I was going to divorce him. He agreed and assumed that he would once again go to local counseling. I put my foot down and said no—he needed to go away for intensive treatment, and it had to be a Christian facility. He found the Begin Again Institute and went.

Oddly enough, I'm going to compliment him now. He's a very good man who believes in God. He's a hard worker and good helpmate. He handles finances well and has created a comfortable life for us. I saw the best of him while we were dating, and I know he's capable of loving me the way God commands a man to love his wife. But, he let the addict have control, and it was destroying him and our marriage. I was not surprised that he was a sexual addict when it was confirmed by the counselor. This was not the man I fell in love with.

As I mentioned earlier, I was reading my book, filling out the workbook, and journaling daily while he was in treatment. I began to understand how sexual addiction can take over someone's life. I also learned that the addict can get to the point of self-hatred because they cannot control themselves. He was so frustrated and miserable that he lashed out at me. I'm not saying his behavior was acceptable—I'm saying that I understand how the addiction changed who he was.

He finished with his therapy and was ready to come home. I was not happy about it. When I picked him up at the airport, it was like Satan himself got in the car. I thought I was going to have a panic attack. I had to put on my fake smile and act like I was kinda-sorta-maybe glad to see him. The tension was unbearable when we got home.

Over the next few days, I could see there was a change in him, and he was trying to respect me. It was a nice change, but I didn't buy it. The man should have been an actor—I knew this show and wasn't interested in more reruns. However, it appeared he was serious about his recovery. His main concern seemed to be what I needed to feel safe. He was soft-spoken and caring. My first thought was, *Ok, who are you and what have you done with my husband?*

Sounds nice and cozy, right? Unfortunately, it didn't take long to catch him in his first lie, which turned into manipulation with an attempt to control. Well, Cat had been studying and learning too while he was gone. He didn't have a chance. I called him out on the lie, and the argument was on. It took about an hour for him to admit he had fallen back into his past behavior, and he apologized. I retracted my cat claws and made dinner. Three more lies surfaced, and I again called him out on each lie before he quickly fessed up. I believe that was the day he learned I will *not* back down and *will* hold him accountable.

My account of his treatment is not complete—I can only share what he chose to tell me. I have seen some substantial changes in him, and it's clear that he's trying hard to work his program. Since old habits die hard, he occasionally struggled with his emotions, but that's understandable. Since I hadn't gone for treatment yet, I was on guard most of the time.

During his treatment, they created a timeline that helped the group understand how the addict was able to manifest itself into their brain. It's like an alien takes over their mind and grows until it gains control. He showed me his timeline, and there were a lot of risk factors in his past that played parts in the addiction.

As a young man, he did not have a loving or close relationship with his father. There was little interaction. His grandparents lived with them while his mother worked, so he was basically raised by his grandmother. The women ran the family. His father basically told him that he had to make his own way in life and rarely complimented him on his accomplishments. Frank is an intelligent man who has the ability to acquire knowledge quickly. He worked at a local refinery and had a well-paying position before he retired.

He was switched on his legs by his mother for several years as a young man. Sometimes the punishment was so severe that his legs bled. I definitely believe you could call that child abuse.

Frank got married right out of high school and allowed his ex-wife to control him, as well as his daughter. He did as he was told to avoid conflict. The ex-wife is no longer in the picture, but the daughter is still controlling.

His ex-wife had numerous affairs and had no interest in being intimate with him. Yet, he stayed with her because he figured that was the best he could do, plus he wanted to be with his child. She was a hateful and demanding person (I've met her and will indeed agree).

There were many other contributing factors, but it became obvious that when he married me, he decided that no woman was ever going to control him again. I'm not a controlling woman, but that didn't matter to him. He came to me broken, and I had no idea what I was getting into.

The facility he attended was situated in the mountains. Each day, the men would spend time outside, which included hiking and getting in touch with nature. They were also taught the technique of meditation.

Frank said one of the toughest segments was when they learned about the pain their addiction has caused their partners. The counselors went into great detail about the possible damages that included loss of self-esteem, poor body image, insecurity, destruction of intimacy, lack of trust, health issues, and many, many more. He said there wasn't a dry eye in the place when they got done with that session.

He shared one other heart-wrenching incident with me. Prior to attending, each man was required to bring a picture of himself as a young boy. They were instructed to look at the picture intensely. Then the counselor asked this question: "Is this what you wanted for that young man?" I can't even imagine the emotion in the room that day. After he told me, it made me look at a picture of myself as a young lady, which made me cry because I knew this certainly wasn't what I wanted for myself.

After he came home, he told me he was glad I pushed him into going. He looked like he'd had the life beat out of him, but that was okay. It was intense, and he learned so much about his addiction. He has the right tools to control it now and appears to be working the program aggressively. He rarely misses a phone meeting or his weekly web-cam call with his counselor and the four other men in the group. These men have formed a close bond and really support each other. He tells me that he's been clean since the day he went in. I would love to believe him, but I can't yet because I still see him as a perpetual liar. He has to earn my trust.

I pray every night that he'll stay the course and destroy the addict. I do love him and am really trying hard to understand his position, but I'm also mentally preparing myself in the event that we don't make it.

PART I: GET OFF MY PORCH

Chapter 5

CAT'S INTENSIVE COUNSELING

Before I get into my counseling experience, I would like to share something of great importance. I had been corresponding with the counselor via email and phone prior to going. I'd been trying to figure out which emotion controlled me the most to have a starting place to work on my anger. I was getting frustrated because I discovered in my book that I had many emotions to deal with, and I felt overwhelmed.

Later on that day, I had a clear vision from God while I was cleaning the house. I didn't think much about it at the time, but as the day went on, it had recurred several times and I wrote it down. I feel that I need to share it with you.

> *I was in a small, empty room with white walls and one chair. I was sitting exactly in the middle of the room against the back wall with my hands crossed in my lap. There were two doors on each side and a large window in front of me. I was intensely staring at the window, and Frank was walking back and forth with an occasional glance my way.*
>
> *Suddenly, the window was gone, and he began to walk very slowly, just a few feet in front of me. He stopped and looked directly at me with a smile. He extended a hand towards me as if to help me out of the chair, but when I reached out to take his hand, the window was back and he was gone. Then there were different men coming in and out of the doors simultaneously. Each one was extending his hand out to me, but I kept trying to see if Frank was still walking behind the window—he wasn't there.*

I dropped my head down and cried. Then I heard footsteps, and once again the window was gone and Frank was walking slowly back and forth in front of me with an occasional glance but no emotion on his face. He stopped and extended his hand out to me again, but when I reached for it, he walked out through one of the doors.

I saw myself sitting in the corner with my head down like a child in time out. A pair of feet appeared out of nowhere underneath my head, and when I looked up, it was Frank. This time he stretched out both hands to me, but when I reached for them he walked out the other door.

I was back crying in time-out. The feet appeared again, and when I looked up it was Frank again. I stood up, looked directly into his eyes, and then I walked out one of the doors. I saw total darkness, and there was a light on the floor that kept moving so I followed it. All at once, the entire area lit up, and I saw countless doors. I began to open them one by one, and behind each door, Frank was standing there laughing at me.

A chair appeared in the middle of the room, and I sat down, dropped my head, closed my eyes, and never looked up again. The feeling was total abandonment.

The next day I spoke with the counselor and read the vision to him. He was pleased that I had typed it out. He said he believed that abandonment is the biggest issue that triggers my anger. That day, I discovered you can live with someone, but that doesn't mean you're not alone.

Before Frank came home, I insisted he take a polygraph test, which he agreed to. I wasn't playing with this man and wanted everything on the table. I'm now going to share those questions and answers with you. You will see one that involves my son.

This is because he and Frank have a close relationship, but Frank had lied to him for years and thrown me under the bus because it was obvious our marriage was not going well. He basically told him I was insecure because I was getting older, was jealous of younger women, and took it out on him. I hadn't told my son about our intimate life because I felt it was inappropriate, so he had no idea I was dealing with a sex addict. It was clear that he believed Frank, which caused me a lot of emotional pain because my son and I have always had a great relationship.

Here are the questions followed by his answers:

1. Since our relationship began until the current date, has he had a physical or sexual relationship with another woman or man? NO.

2. Since our relationship began until the current date, has he had an emotional relationship with another woman? NO.

3. Has he ever watched child pornography? NO.

4. Does he currently have a separate bank account, investment, or money that I am not aware of? NO.

5. Does he currently have a computer or any other electronic device in our home (other than the one in the office, my tablet, and cell phones) that I am not aware of? NO.

6. Is he connected to the Internet on his cell phone? YES, *but he has never accessed it and can prove it.*

7. Does he currently possess any form of pornographic material anywhere on the property where we reside or in his truck? NO.

8. Has he made a purchase of pornographic nature since we've been married? NO.

9. Is he still lying to my son and blaming me for the marital problems we've been having? NO.

10. Has he told my son the absolute truth about how he has abused me? YES.

11. Does he have a secret email account that I'm not aware of? NO.

12. Does he find my body undesirable? NO.

13. Has he been lying to me when he says he truly looks past the imperfections of my body? NO.

I'm happy to report that he passed the test. The day he completed his therapy, my son picked him up so he could spend an additional week with him to decompress. He took the polygraph two days after he completed the program. He confessed everything to my son the day he picked him up because he had no access to phones while in treatment.

The last two questions of the polygraph were eye-openers for me. I really thought if he answered no he was going to get caught lying because his behavior didn't reflect his true feelings. But what it taught me was that he had given the addict full control to the point where he was unable to have a normal and healthy sex life.

Three weeks after Frank came home, I went for my private counseling. When he dropped me off at the airport, he approached me for a hug. I was so angry that I just turned and walked away. I couldn't believe that I had to be counseled again (for about the fifth or sixth time). His addiction had threatened my health and state of mind. I hated him so much that I prayed he'd be gone when I got back (not "dead gone," just gone). I never wanted to see him again—I had been a good wife and didn't deserve this. While on the plane, I thought about my life with him, which ticked me off even more. Needless to say, I was not in a good mood when I reached my destination.

When I walked into the counselor's office, I knew I was done—I was on a mission. I had three days of four-hour sessions that I attended. The counselor had brought in a female associate who had been through a situation similar to mine. It was good to know that I was not alone. She understood what I was going through and gave me good advice. Looking back, I believe she was an angel sent from God, and even today she follows up with my progress.

The male counselor explained to me in great detail how the addict's behavior affected my brain, which caused PTSD. He was one of the kindest men I've ever met. I have to say he and the female associate were top-notch, and I was comfortable with them.

During my counseling session, I discovered that I had allowed the addict to change who I was. The following is a list of emotions I experienced regularly:

- Anger
- Loneliness
- Hurt
- Rejection
- Helplessness
- Insecurity
- Inadequacy
- Insignificance
- Hostility

- Isolation
- Frustration
- Embarrassment
- Depression
- Loss of control
- Numbness
- Emptiness
- Disconnected
- Hollowness
- Knotted
- Rage
- Uncontrolled crying
- Constricted
- Emotionally bruised
- Sensitivity
- Tense/Tight
- Shaky
- Suffocation
- Drained
- Confusion

- Discouragement
- Distant
- Stupid
- Anxiety
- Overwhelmed
- Apathetic
- Irritation
- Skeptical
- Critical
- Hatefulness
- Ashamed
- Boredom
- Sadness

Lord have mercy, I was the poster child for PTSD!

I also received an education on why Frank acted out with sexual behavior. Since I'm not a sex addict, I don't totally understand, but I think it could be applicable to an alcoholic, an overeater, or other addictions. The behavior could be the result of anxiety, anger, empty feelings, rage, shame, fear, powerlessness, embarrassment, guilt, or other unresolved issues from the past, like the items in his timeline.

I didn't think I would be able to pity him, but now I do. It's so sad that his chances for a good relationship were affected by other people's influences. When we're growing up, we look to our parents and siblings for guidance and tend to take those traits into our adult life. Unfortunately, he didn't get what he needed and felt he had to compensate for his inadequacies.

I also found out that Frank is a narcissist. I had a lot of names for him, but that wasn't one of them. When I thought about it, it made sense. He's egotistical and uses his intelligence as a weapon. He can't be wrong, and he'll fight to the end to win an argument. He's actually lied about a subject he had no knowledge of to look more intelligent.

Even though I feel sorry for him, I can't let that affect my own recovery. My anger has come down substantially now that I understand how he became an addict. He has the tools to fight the addiction now, so he has no one to blame but himself if he fails.

The knowledge I received was amazing. I learned that it was not my fault and I deserve to be treated with dignity and respect. They made me realize it was okay to be selfish and do whatever was necessary to recover. They were so gentle and caring opposed to the counselors I had previously seen who were all business.

Well, it was time for me to go home, and I wasn't ready for it. I had to tell Frank he needed to leave again. The addict had forced me to make a decision between staying together in the same house and risking a setback in my health or being alone and recovering. Regardless of the progress he was making, I knew I couldn't work my program and recover while living in the same house. I know he would try to counsel me, and that would not work. He needed to stay focused on his own program.

Now, Frank no longer lives here—he had to go. He's not in a hotel or at a buddy's house this time. He bought a house that we can use as rental property if this marriage is able to survive. If not, he'll have a nice place to live. I told him there's only one King and he's not it. When he walked away from God, he walked away from me.

PART I: GET OFF MY PORCH

I knew without a doubt that I could never recover if we lived together. My path is clear, and I'll not let anything or anyone stand in my way. I'm happy to report that I am once again playing the piano, singing while I clean the house, playing more with my dog, working on my self-esteem, and feeling better every day.

Before he moved out, Frank composed a very touching poem for me, which I would like to share.

FRANK'S POEM

"We stand upon the shore of a violent land
Looking back, we see the devastation behind us
Looking ahead, we see the ocean where we stand
We know we must leave this place
Unsure of where our destination leads
Only knowing to follow God's face
He has supplied our two small ships
We must do this journey together but apart
We set out with our dreams and hopes
As we go, I watch over and protect you
Knowing your journey is yours
But ever waiting for whatever God needs me to do
When you are strong, I stand back and cheer you on
When you are tired or weak I pull your ship with mine
In the distance we see the place
Our Godly destination

We enter our new land with great expectation
You see the real me for the first time
You feel confident, secure, and protected
Finally letting go of all that was behind
We move forward together
To a place we've never been before
A place of trust, a place of faith
A place of love, a place of grace"

Yes, it made me cry. I know he loves me and is going through the biggest battle of his life. He's definitely able to make it if he chooses. But he needs to gag the addict and knock him off his shoulder in order to stay connected to God.

PART I: GET OFF MY PORCH

Chapter 6

THE PEACEFUL SEPARATION

Are you in shock by the title of this chapter? I found out that it is possible to have a peaceful separation. I know what it feels like to really love someone. Unfortunately, Frank does not, but he's finding out. Since I do love him (but hate the addict), I decided I would bite the bullet and learn more about sexual addiction. It was disturbing, but I realized I needed to step outside of my own pain and do some research. I don't believe I can make a final decision about the marriage until I understand what I'm dealing with.

In layman's terms, this is some of the information I found about sexual addiction:

- It's seen as a disease and not a moral flaw.

- It can alter the brain's capacity to think rationally.

- The addict engages in compulsive behaviors not for pleasure but to relieve distress or pain.

- Many addicts grew up in toxic families and have a hard time trusting others.

- There may have been trauma during adulthood or childhood that has not been dealt with.

- People can inherit a genetic predisposition to an addiction.

- The addiction could be a result of physical or sexual abuse, rejection, or abandonment.

- Their parents didn't exhibit a good, loving relationship.

- The male figure in their life disrespected women and saw them as objects, not people.

- Media's exploitation of women plays a role.

- The addict did not have a good moral compass.

- The addict may have had a controlling spouse.

- The addict had experienced or experiences insecurity.

This list has helped me put some things in perspective. I've picked out the ones I know are applicable to Frank and will provide an explanation:

- *It's seen as a disease and not a moral flaw*: He loves God and has good morals. He gets so frustrated because he knows it is wrong and destroying our marriage, but he can't control it.

- *It can alter the brain's capacity to think rationally*: When he fails and gives in to the addiction, there is extreme remorse because he is an intelligent man and should be able to stop himself.

- *The addict engages in compulsive behaviors not for pleasure but to relieve distress or pain*: His anger and frustration with the addiction and the pain he's caused me creates extreme stress.

- *There may have been trauma during adulthood or childhood that has not been dealt with*: When he was a young boy, his mother whipped him with a switch, and there were times his legs bled.

- *Physical or sexual abuse*: Again, the whippings.

- *Rejection*: His father loved him but didn't spend time with him or provide guidance into adulthood. His ex-wife had many affairs and was not interested in him sexually. His ex-girlfriend that I mentioned earlier used him then threw him away. He was rejected by most of the girls in high school.

- *Abandonment*: He was abandoned by his father, ex-wife, and ex-girlfriend.

- *Their parents didn't exhibit a good, loving relationship*: His parents showed little affection for each other.

- *The male figure in their life disrespected women and saw them as objects, not people*: His father objectified women terribly, even in front of him and his mother.

- *Media's exploitation of women*: I think this one speaks for itself.

- *The addict did not have a good moral compass*: His father displayed behavior that suggested objectification of women was the norm and it was okay to disrespect your wife.

- *A controlling spouse*: His ex-wife, daughter, and ex-girlfriend totally controlled him.

- *Insecurity*: How could he not be insecure? When we got married, he had decided that no woman would ever control him again, so here I sit writing a book about sexual addiction.

No wonder he came to me so messed up! But let me be clear when I say, *this does not excuse what he's done to me*. I fought him from the newlywed stage until last August of 2017 trying to make him stop. I threatened to divorce him many times, I begged, I pleaded, I pitched him out for seven months, we went to counselors, and nothing worked. The only thing I got out of the marriage was a horrible sickness. *I paid the price for his addiction with my health!*

There were a lot of discussions that led up to the separation instead of a divorce. Before I went to counseling, I had drawn up a divorce contract in the event we didn't make it and set up a safety deposit box with additional papers I would need. Frank agreed and signed it. I believe he did so because he thought I would change my mind before I came back. Well, that didn't work out so well for him because the morning after I got back, I presented the contract to him and told him I definitely wanted a divorce.

Living alone sounded great to me because I could create my own atmosphere, safety, and happiness. I used to have the attitude that I would stay and roll with the punches because of my age, the pain of divorce, and starting over again, but I decided being alone would be far better than living with a man who had so little respect for me that he would rather live with his sin than honor the marriage vows and treat me the way God intended. My goal was to do what was necessary to get my emotions and health under control. He had emotionally beaten me down for the last time, and I intended to take back the control I've allowed him to have. The bad news is that I am responsible for damage control after the havoc the addict caused to my health. But there's one thing I know for sure—I know God loves me more than Frank ever will, and His plan for me is peace, joy, and comfort.

I learned in counseling that I am not to blame for his addiction (i.e., "Was I a good wife?" "Was it my fault because I had aged and gained some weight?" "Did I pay enough attention to him?" "Did he grow tired of me?") I can say without reservation that I was a great wife, but with a sex addict, it doesn't matter.

PART I: GET OFF MY PORCH

When he came home from therapy, it felt like a bank robber had been released from jail and was coming to live with me. I use the term bank robber because of all he's stolen from me: my self-worth, peace, security, trust, intimacy, and sex life. Home had been my sanctuary for over two weeks, and I was an emotional wreck knowing that he was coming back.

He did take the blame for causing my pain, but that didn't make me feel loved or safe. I honestly believed he wanted me to go for therapy (now I'm really glad I did) so he could feel like he did his job to undo the mess he created, which would be an easy fix for him. But his job is to behave his way back, earn the trust that he destroyed, and take the necessary steps to make me feel loved and safe. What he didn't understand before therapy is that I didn't trust him with my heart or health.

We decided to wait until January of 2018 before we put our plan into action because we had family visiting for the holidays. The holidays were a bit stressful, but we made it. It was obvious that he was extremely upset, but I was ready to put my life back together. In order to calm him down, I explained that we were toxic to each other's recovery because I'd be waiting for that other shoe to drop and he'd be afraid of unwarranted suspicion on my part. Since he was controlling and arrogant, he would assume the position of counselor and I would have to report my progress to him. Plus, I knew he was a liar, and it's hard to have an adult conversation with a habitual liar.

He started looking for a house right away and was out by the 26th of January. During that time, I started thinking about what he'd gone through before we met and realized that I hadn't even given him a chance to use his tools to recover. I softened up and told him I would be willing to separate and have a contract in the event it didn't work out. Needless to say, that took a lot of stress off the situation.

I'm happy to report that we are doing very well so far. We're actually dating and talk or see each other daily. I went with him to pick out some new furniture and helped organize and decorate his house. We've had a couple of "spats" but were able to resolve them quickly.

He seems determined to earn my trust. He asked me to put blocks on his TV, and he does not have a computer or tablet. He has a flip-phone (yes, he's old fashioned), and I have the freedom to check it any time to see if he has activated the Internet (which he's never done). Along with not carrying cash, he will keep every receipt for the money he spends to alleviate my concerns about what he purchases, and we will balance the checkbook together. He gave me a key to the house and permission to come in whenever I please. This was all his idea.

I was not comfortable with it at first because I didn't want to micromanage him and thought he should have the ability to control things himself. I tend to forget that he's still a work in progress, and he said he really needs my help.

Frank had a great idea. He'd read about a reward system and suggested that we use it to gain my trust. So, I bought a large glass jar and some pretty blue rocks. Each time he is considerate, loving, caring, attentive, respectful, and all the other good stuff a husband's supposed to be, I put a rock in the jar. He had earned twenty-five, but then he lied (which I will always confront him about). He owned the lie and apologized, but now Frank only has twenty rocks. When he gets one hundred, I will treat him to a steak dinner. This may sound silly to some people, but over time, he's learning new behaviors that will hopefully become good habits.

Hopefully, together we can destroy the demon. He still appears to be seriously working the program and rarely misses a group meeting or phone conference. We have had a good start, but I'm aware that things could change in the blink of an eye if he doesn't stay the course and be vigilant every day. If he allows the addict to control him again, there will be a divorce.

This plan would not work for everyone, but we know it's the best one for us. I'm aware that I could be setting him up for failure because he's living alone, but I'd rather be apart if he doesn't make it. He created this mess, and it's his job to clean it up. I know he can do it, but whether he does or not is totally up to him. As for me, I'm going to be just fine either way.

The most important person I'll ever be in a relationship with is myself.

Chapter 7

A LETTER TO THE ADDICTION

In the book *Facing Heartbreak* by Stephanie Carnes, Mari A. Lee and Anthony D. Rodriguez, I ran across an amazing letter to "Sex Addiction" from a woman named Amy, who is the wife of a sex addict. This letter[1] was my breakthrough! I cannot even begin to tell you how it empowered me to stand up and fight to take my control back. I will quote it as written with the exception of how long we've been married and the name at the end, which personalizes it for me. I have printed out a copy for myself and read it often.

> Sex Addiction:
>
> You are a rotten disgusting plague, and I am now choosing to heal from you once and for all. In doing so, I would like you to know what your role and influence in my husband's life has done to me. Because of you, sex addiction, and the way <u>you</u> took advantage of his pain, I began to feel fat, ugly, and stupid. Because of you, sex addiction, I hated my husband; I hit him and screamed names at him that I would not call my worst enemy. What I know now is that YOU are my worst enemy. You are the silent slithering snake of addiction that lurks in the hearts and minds of so many hurting men and women and even children in this world. You seduce and ensnare, you promise all kinds of things that are outright lies, and you dangle yourself through the Internet, through clubs, magazines, Craig's List, shows, movies, strip clubs, and massage parlors. You offer false comfort. You are a liar, a cheat, a

PART I: GET OFF MY PORCH

disease maker, a heart breaker, and a booby trap. You steal the hopes and dreams of couples everywhere. You break people down into little more than liars and snoops, you try to change the blueprint of people, and you turn us into the harpies and the henpecked of the world.

Sex addiction, you almost won. For 19 years now you have stolen my joy, my comfort, and the sexual energy that was supposed to be for my husband and I. You made me feel like an unlovable fool.

BUT NO MORE

As of today, I am breaking your hold on my heart and mind. I will no longer give you power and control over my emotions. You will no longer be my obsession, my every waking thought. I will no longer allow you to pull me around by my nose— constantly worried, angry, and upset. I will no longer be your slave in snooping, comparing, lying, and crying.

I am BREAKING your hold on me. I AM taking back MY power.

You will die and shrivel away from lack of energy because I am taking my life back again. I cannot speak for my husband, I cannot control his choices, I hope with time and healing that he will put you in your grave, but I will no longer allow you to whisper in my ear to try to control him, I cannot and will not. BUT, I can control my choices moving forward. I KNOW that I have hurts that need to be healed, and as long as I keep blaming and shaming my husband, I will stay stuck in your insidious plan forever. I have given you a lot...too much! I have given you my self-esteem, my sanity, and my sexuality, but I will NOT give you my forever. And I

WILL now reclaim who I am in the world. I am sure you will try and tempt me to go back into my old codependent ways, and I know it will not be easy some days. But I want you to hear this loud and clear:

YOU DO NOT CONTROL MY JOY, MY HAPPINESS, MY HOPE, MY CHOICES, MY HEALING, OR MY LIFE ANY LONGER, SEX ADDICTION. I AM THROUGH WITH YOU.

With determination and dignity,

Cat

Needless to say, I cried my eyes out after reading this. Amy is my hero. She said it in such a way that put me in attack mode. While I was just typing the letter from Amy, I decided that I would also make a copy, give it to Frank, and ask him to read it once a week (which I hope he will do) so that he can be reminded that this "silent slithering snake" can be destroyed.

I suggest you read her letter as many times as it takes to make you *very angry*, then use that anger to heal yourself. You're a child of God and deserve to be happy.

---

[1]From *Facing Heartbreak: Steps to Recovery for Partners of Sex Addicts* by Stefanie Carnes, Mari A. Lee, and Anthony D. Rodriguez. (c) 2012 Gentle Path Press. Edited and reprinted with permission granted by Gentle Path Press and Stefanie Carnes Ph.D., Da, International Institute of Trauma and Addiction Professionals (ITAP), PO Box 2112, Carefree, Arizona 85377.

PART I: GET OFF MY PORCH

Chapter 8

FRANK'S DESTRUCTIVE BEHAVIOR

I briefly talked about the picture of Frank as a child that he took to treatment. We have a family picture displayed in our home from when he was the same age, and after he told me why they requested it, I focused on the image of that little boy. He was such a cute kid—big brown eyes and a sweet little smile. He's wearing black dress pants, a white dress shirt, a tie, and a pullover sweater. He looked like a child model in a catalog—such a little gentleman! I'm sure he dreamed of growing up to be a superhero or astronaut like most little boys do.

I have two sons, and as they grew up, their dreams changed constantly. My oldest son was one of those take-it-apart-and-put-it-back-together kids, and now he has a great career in heating and cooling and built one of the toughest Jeeps in Colorado, starting with just the frame. He's a single dad and has done a fantastic job. My youngest was a police scout at the age of fourteen until he went into the Marines and became a military police officer. After his stint, he moved back to his hometown, grabbed a security job for a short time, became an officer at a local police department, and is now Chief of Police at the age of forty. He married a wonderful woman and has two daughters. The interests I saw in them as children became their realities, and I'm so proud of them. Don't get me wrong—we weren't the Brady Bunch. They were boisterous little boys who gave us a run for our money, but we did the best we could to support their interests and encourage them. Our home was the hub of activity, and their friends loved hanging out there.

Unfortunately, Frank didn't have that type of upbringing, support, or encouragement. He lived in a home with four adults. He had a best friend and spent as much time as he could at his house, where the parents were involved with their children.

Frank had to make his own way in life, but he achieved success in the oil industry despite his shortcomings.

However, the addict in him was busy during his adult life. Frank was extremely unhappy in his first marriage. He allowed his wife (who had many affairs) to control him, and he had a daughter who took after mom and controlled him, a pitiful sex life, and not much of a social life. He was a hard worker and made decent money, but she spent it as quickly as he made it. She divorced him for two years and played around with a few guys. I assume she discovered she couldn't be the queen with them, so she lured Frank back in. He married her again, only because he wanted to be with his daughter.

The second marriage was also a disaster because she continued to cheat on him. He became depressed and hated life. She once again wanted out, and divorce papers were in order before their daughter went to college. Frank was finally free to find a good woman, but in the meantime, the addict had gained full control. If it sounds like I'm making excuses for Frank's behavior, I'm not. But I *am* pointing out the *reasons* he was such an easy target for sexual addiction.

People use the word "hate" in their vocabulary, but have they really thought about what they're saying? *Hate* defined by Merriam-Webster means "intense hostility and aversion derived from fear, anger, or sense of injury; loathing; to feel extreme enmity towards." Now, let's have a look at the word *enmity*, which means "positive, active, and typically mutual hatred or ill will; hostility, antipathy, antagonism, animosity, rancor." That is exactly how I felt about Frank, so I did indeed hate the dude. But, I don't anymore because I got an education about his addiction.

As you know by now, I'm a Christian and love God. I love deeply and have a lot of compassion, even with those who have hurt me physically or emotionally, because I don't know their story or what they may be going through. I wasn't born that way—I'm into self-help and improvement books because I want to please God and be happy even through adversities.

Then along came Frank. I hung on to my marital vows, stayed close to God, and tried to keep my loving, understanding, and "Proverbs Wife" status as long as I could, but I'd met my match with the addict. Over the years of emotional abuse, I gradually became an angry, hateful, insecure woman. I despised the ground he walked on and didn't like myself much either. On the contrary, I was able to be myself with everybody else. I couldn't quite figure out why, then realized I didn't trust him with my heart and that he had become the enemy.

I truly believe there are heartless and cruel people in the world who could care less about the path of destruction they leave behind. An addict has the same type of personality and behavior. Here's how I would describe Frank:

- Tense
- Narcissistic
- Controlling
- Selfish
- Manipulative
- Liar
- Conceited
- Abusive
- Incapable of loving
- Egotistical
- Hostile

- Anger
- Apathetic
- Isolated
- Inferior
- Distant
- Sarcastic
- Frustrated
- Judgmental
- Depressed
- Hateful
- Critical
- Dark
- Disconnected
- Empty
- Blocked
- Dull

Here's how I would describe myself *before* I met him:

- Content
- Thoughtful
- Intimate

PART I: GET OFF MY PORCH

- Loving
- Trusting
- Nurturing
- Faithful
- Appreciated
- Respectful
- Relaxed
- Peaceful
- Secure
- Thankful
- Grateful
- Worthwhile
- Confident
- Responsible
- Discerning
- Successful
- Creative
- Joyful
- Optimistic
- Playful

- Hopeful
- Energetic
- Cheerful

Sounds like a recipe for disaster, right? Well, it was, but in my defense, those were not the behaviors he exhibited before we got married. As you know, everyone puts their best foot forward in the wooing stage. What I'd seen was a different man. But the addict is sly indeed. Over the years he slowly took me down, and suddenly I realized my health and sanity were in real danger. I was the boiling frog, but I jumped out just in time to save myself. I should have never let him come back after the first separation, but once again, he played me and I fell for it.

Never underestimate the addict that resides in your loved one. They will take you down with no remorse whatsoever. It won't bother them to see you in pain, and your threats *do not* scare them. They may be concerned for a while but also have the ability to play the victim and get you back in line. *Addicts are master manipulators!* Here's a few of the many lines Frank had used:

- "I don't know why you stay with me—I'm such a loser."
- "You could have picked anyone but me—I don't deserve you."
- "I deserve any punishment you dish out because I'm so stupid."
- "God gave me a beautiful woman, and I've treated you so badly."
- "I love you so much—you're beautiful inside and out—from the top of your head to the bottom of your feet."
- "I've been praying and getting closer to God, and I'm so sorry...I'll never hurt you again."

- "God got ahold of me, and I'm going to treat you as He commands."

- "I'm not worthy of your love—you deserve so much better."

This is just a short list, and I'm sure you've heard similar things. But notice that they label *themselves* to get your sympathy: "I'm a loser, I don't deserve you, I'm so stupid, I've treated you badly, I'm not worthy of your love." Have you noticed that when they say those things, you immediately reassure them they're not like that? I sure did. They'll cry, put on a sad face, drop their chin down, give you the puppy dog eyes, or my all-time favorite: hit themselves on the head. You actually start feeling sorry for them! Looking back, I wish I would have smacked him right in the kisser, but I didn't realize I was being manipulated until late in the marriage (wow, Gramma's getting a little feisty in her old age! Grandpa left just in time).

I'm about to get real personal and tell you about some of the most damaging ways he abused me. I haven't been looking forward to this part of the book, but I feel it's necessary to let you know you're not the only one. It would take time to list everything, but these are some of the ugly ones. I have no doubt that some of you have been through much worse, but the end result is the same—you're in terrible pain and see no way out except divorce. Just keep in mind it's the addict that takes over. I'm not making excuses for the way Frank treated me, but I understand more since I've had counseling.

While we were dating, he brought a pornographic movie over. I don't watch the nasty things, but I was "in love" (more like "in stupid") and reluctantly said okay. It didn't take long for me to let him know I wasn't that kind of girl, so he obliged and said he wasn't into it either but a friend gave it to him to see if it would "spice things up" for us. (That was the first red flag I missed.)

I mentioned earlier that Frank had lost interest in me sexually after the first three months of marriage. He worked an early shift, and if I got up to use the restroom before he left, I was ushered back to bed because I "needed my sleep." I had no idea what was going on in the living room during his morning ritual. He didn't hear me get up one morning, and I saw him "acting out" while watching half-naked women on the beach. I was totally devastated but didn't confront him because I had enough problems on my plate already. I assumed that's what he did since he'd been single for a long time but he'd stop if I approached him more often sexually. Needless to say, that didn't work either.

When I first met Frank, we started attending church together. I looked forward to going and became active in the help ministry. After we got married, I noticed he spent most of his time checking out the women in church, and he wasn't making any attempt to hide it from me. I've seen a lot of those perverted men in my life, and they're very obvious. Not only did he hurt me emotionally, but he was an embarrassment. We haven't been to church in several years. He couldn't even stop objectifying women long enough to worship God.

During our entire marriage, he rarely complimented me on my appearance and *never* told me I was sexy (which a wife needs to hear occasionally). I'm far from ugly and am always well-groomed. I used to compliment him a lot on his appearance, especially when he dressed up. If the occasion called for elegance, I spent a lot of time on my hair, makeup, and wardrobe. I thought I looked quite lovely, but the most I got (which wasn't often) was, "You look nice." Usually, he just said, "You ready?" To be honest, I *still* get hit on by other men—some of them much younger than I am—but I couldn't seem to get my own husband's attention.

Over time, I gave up—he wasn't worth it. I dress nicely and wear makeup when I go out in public, but all Frank gets now is frumpy sweats with an oversized shirt. I don't wear sexy lingerie anymore—it's big night shirts. Almost all the clothes I wear around him are black so I can hide my imperfections. I wear nothing alluring to tempt him because I know it won't matter, but that's okay because I have absolutely no desire to be with him intimately. I gave up shorts in the summertime and suffered the heat because that's his favorite time of year to objectify women and I don't have a chance. When I sit down, the pillow goes right in my lap (some of you know what I'm talking about, don't you?) He had totally destroyed my body image and made me feel ashamed of myself.

When it came to division of labor, I was considerate and thanked him for his help around the house or a project he'd done. I will say he was good about helping if I asked. I've always done all the housework and kept an immaculate house, cooked good meals, did all the laundry and a lot of the yard work, washed my own car, cleaned off the patio, ran errands, and countless other wifely duties before I retired and after. I did more than my share with very little thanks from him.

When he came home from work, he didn't have to do *anything*. His ritual consisted of coming in the door, ignoring me most of the time, complaining about work, going downstairs to work out for an hour, coming upstairs again to complain some more, and then watch television. I continued on with my duties and cooked dinner. I usually made his plate and delivered it to him while he was sitting on the couch. Most often, he gulped his food down with no compliments to the cook, and then I collected his plate and went back to the kitchen.

Sounds like a man's idea of the perfect wife doesn't it? But wait, there's more! After dinner, he usually took a shower and plopped back down on the couch to finish his ritual of ignoring me and watching television. There was rarely any mention of spending time with me in the bedroom. I didn't ask and didn't complain.

I don't know if a sex addict feels any guilt about not taking care of his partner, but he started using some really stupid tactics to avoid being with me. He tried to convince me that he had erectile dysfunction, which I could confirm he did not. Since that didn't work, he tried performance anxiety (which he may have had because of his fantasies about other women). In my research, I discovered that men will use erectile dysfunction and performance anxiety to have an excuse to not be with their partner. They deceive, lie, and seek sympathy for conditions that do not exist so they won't be pressured by their partners.

His next tactic was to convince me that he was upset because he loved me so much and was afraid to be intimate with me because he felt like a failure (the sympathy card). I played the good wife and convinced him that he was not a failure. He shot himself in the foot on that one because now he felt obligated. Then he put the other foot in his mouth and said, "As long as I look at your face, it helps me focus on you." I suppose he thought that was a compliment, but what I heard was, "As long as I don't have to look at your imperfect body, I can perform." I guess I don't need to tell you that statement still hurts me to this day. I don't know if I will ever be able to forgive him for saying that. That was when I lost what little respect I had left for him in the bedroom.

Here's the final tactic he used until he went to treatment. Almost every night between seven and eight he started yawning very loud and announced that he was exhausted. However, he was able to stay up and watch television until ten and talked so much that I wasn't able to hear or stay focused on what we were watching. I know what my husband looks like when he's tired, and he was lying to me probably eighty percent of the time. I don't know why this performance was necessary because I hadn't asked for sex in years. Maybe he was trying to make sure that he kept me in line.

A few years ago, I ended up in the emergency room because I had a major break out and my throat was closing up. While they were working on me, I watched him objectify the nurses, and he paid little attention to what was going on. I was hospitalized and kept as an in-patient. The first night they gave me Xanax, Prednisone, antibiotics, and a sleeping pill. I'm into all natural things, so my body had an adverse reaction. I had a "night terror" and fell out of bed. I had no recollection of falling, but they found me several hours later (they obviously weren't keeping an eye on me).

The next morning when I attempted to get up and use the restroom, a nurse came in and instructed me to stay in bed because my hip may have been broken due to a fall. They had a sensor alert on my bed. I immediately called Frank, and he came right up. A rather attractive nurse explained to him what had happened, and of course, the patient (me) didn't get much attention. She told him I'd be going for X-rays shortly. Well, after the nurse left, Frank quickly informed me that he had to go back to work and followed her. He never came back to hear the results or comfort me.

The X-rays came out okay, so I called him at work. He seemed happy that my hip wasn't broken, but the conversation was short because he was too "busy." He didn't show much concern for me. He came up again after work. Of course, he had to check out the eye candy, which added to my anxiety. I told him I had to stay a couple more days for observation. He was the last person I wanted to see, and I couldn't wait for him to leave when he visited. Needless to say, I was an emotional wreck by the time I was discharged. I'd like to say I was used to the objectification by now, but it never ceased to hurt.

I was sent home with a lot of medication, as well as a nebulizer and Wellbutrin, so there was a schedule I had to follow. I was groggy and disoriented and slept a lot. I assumed that he'd be there to take care of me for a few days because it was very traumatic, but he went right back to work the next day.

I was alone, drugged up, and weak, and I had trouble breathing and difficulty walking because of the pain in my hip. I was afraid to use the stove so ate very little, and I was depressed. I had to set a timer for my meds every four hours. The first time I attempted to take them, I spilled a couple of bottles on the floor and had to get down on my knees to pick them up. I remember taking pills, but to this day I have no idea how many or which ones I took—I could have overdosed. However, he was kind enough to give me the correct dosages after he got home. The next day I threw the meds in the trash with the exception of the Prednisone and antibiotic because I seriously needed them. I still had to use the nebulizer and missed several treatments.

He continued to work, and over time I became more alert and better able to take care of myself. I spent most of my time on the couch during my recovery. My entertainment was watching him watch young, provocative women on TV. He didn't pay much attention to me but took care of my needs when he was there. Once I got well, my miserable life went on as usual. I've learned that when I'm sick, he does only what's necessary because I'm of no use to him. However, he demands a lot of attention from me when he doesn't feel well.

Frank played a huge part in my development of insomnia. After I caught him acting out in the living room when we were newlyweds, a good night's sleep became just a memory. If I had to use the restroom, I stayed in the bedroom until he left because the living room was right outside the door. There were many times that I was literally in pain because I held my water too long.

When Frank lived here before the separation, I quickly learned to listen before I left the bedroom because I knew there was always a possibility I'd catch him. I didn't want to ruin my day before it even started. If I knew he was acting out and I was thirsty, I just got a drink out of the bathroom faucet. On weekends, I would stay in the private area of the master bedroom for an hour after I woke up sometimes because I just didn't want to be around him.

Early in the marriage, I went to the doctor and got a prescription for Zolpidem, which is a sleeping pill, and I used it nightly for over six years. After one pill didn't do the trick, I started using two. It really affected my coordination and thinking process, and my muscles became extremely weak. I was in a stupor most of the time, and my reflexes weren't good. I jumped many a curb while driving, but miraculously, no one was injured and the car was not damaged.

I worked full time at a local health club for fifteen years and was a certified personal trainer and the Director of Aerobics. I personally taught about ten classes a week (three being in a swimming pool), choreographed training videos, was featured in a local commercial, and did sales. My job as a personal trainer required the examination of clients' medical records and creating their programs. The programs consisted of weight room training, cardiovascular machines, and the Nautilus circuit. I also did follow-up rehabilitation with disabled clients according to the doctor's instructions. I was particular and meticulous with each and every client.

Over the years, I became a popular commodity in the area and was approached by other health clubs who wanted to employ me. I was a familiar face in the newspapers and the commercial. After I left my full-time job, I went to work at another health club part time. I did personal training and taught yoga. For those of you who haven't experienced the beauty of yoga, it requires concentration, balance, and breathing techniques. At the risk of sounding conceited, I am proud to say that I excelled in my field and loved what I did. The best part was my ability to help people.

For those of you who believe in God or a higher power, I now realize there's no way I could have had such a successful career while in a drug-induced state without His help. The sleeping pills were extremely powerful (especially when taking a double dose), and the effects remained with me throughout the day. It's scary to think that my clients' safety and well-being was in my hands. I didn't just tell them what to do—I demonstrated every weight lifting move, form, and cardio machine, and I instructed high-impact aerobics, step-aerobics, and a myriad of other things that could have been dangerous not only to the client but to myself.

Eventually, the sleeping pills caught up with me, and my body started a downward spiral. Being the researcher I am, I found out they were addictive, and, if taken over a long period of time, dangerous. So I did what any fool would do—I just stopped taking them. Bad choice—my body was not happy about losing its addictive friend. I wasn't able to walk most mornings for about twenty minutes because my legs gave out. My mind was so confused that I couldn't perform simple tasks or think clearly. I finally came to my senses and found out that I had to gradually reduce the dosage, and over time I was able to stop taking them.

Once again, sleep was rare, so I decided to take melatonin, which is a natural herb. I did fine for a few months, but then my body decided it didn't like that either. So, I turned to an over-the-counter sleep aid to take with my melatonin. I thought that was a good decision but realized I was once again addicted. Now, I take just melatonin and see what happens each night. The addict even stole my right for a peaceful night's sleep.

Since I was so ashamed of my body, I showered before Frank got home from work. I really missed my evening showers because they were relaxing and helped me sleep. The weekends were difficult when he was home. I've had many panic attacks while in the shower because I was afraid he'd come in. After he retired, I had to set boundaries. I shut the door to the master bedroom and told him he needed to stay out. I'm embarrassed to admit that he even controlled my personal hygiene. If I'd felt loved, walking around naked shouldn't have mattered. Frank has not seen me naked for probably eighteen years.

When I got home from a California trip in 2016, I knew something had happened the minute I walked into the house. Frank seemed unsettled and overly attentive. For the next three days, beautiful vases of flowers were delivered. He only occasionally gives me flowers, so this was totally out of character.

He didn't approach me sexually for over a month, and when he did—let's just say something was very wrong with the family jewels. Of course, I noticed and questioned him about it. He said he'd told me he went to an urologist a few months ago and the doctor said it was not an uncommon condition for a man his age. Of course he lied and tried to convince me that I just forgot. I believe I would have remembered that! He eventually admitted that he got "carried away" while acting out when I was gone. So now the addict decided that my sex life (what little there was of it) was over. I don't recall being asked if I was ready for that. I assumed my body would let me know. He has since been to a specialist, and there are options that may repair the damage.

Frank gave me nothing in the bedroom except heartache, and my intimacy tank was empty. Unfortunately, I eventually found *myself* objectifying men and realized I was looking for intimacy and love. I know for a fact that given the chance, I would have had an affair. Thank God above that I prayed myself out of that idea. If I would have followed through, I would have allowed his addiction to lead me into sin. My behavior was the result of abandonment. I don't believe the addict even thinks about the possibility of their partner stepping out of the marriage, but they leave us desperate, which is a dangerous place to be.

I have to wrap up this chapter now even though there's so much more to tell because it's starting to stress me out. Thinking and writing about his destructive behavior is bringing up visuals and emotions that may trigger my PTSD, so I have to be careful. I need to guard my health to prevent a setback. Frank has been gone for almost three weeks now, and I'm doing quite well. I have a long way to go, but I'm going to beat this thing. My immune system has improved substantially, but I'm not where I need to be yet. I lived with a selfish man for over nineteen years, and now it's time for me to be selfish.

When an addict gets total control, the consequences can be deadly. He's ashamed and remorseful and seems determined to put his life back together. We may not make it, but I'll *never* be put in this position again. I stayed there way too long because I loved him, but he wasn't there at all—the addict was.

I can't say that I've forgiven Frank yet, but I know I will. It's going to take some time because he's done so much. Forgiving someone who has treated you so badly with no remorse is difficult because it feels like you're saying what they did to you was okay when it's not. But sometimes you need to dissolve the relationship and move on.

Forgiveness can be for yourself because you take away their power to control your emotions. I've found out that forgiving people for their ignorance works well, but in this case, I can't do that because it's an addiction and is going to take a lot of time and work on both our parts.

To *not* forgive can cause a lot of unnecessary heartache and stress. It's like drinking poison and expecting the other person to die or being in a prison cell with the key in your hand but refusing to let yourself out.

Now that I understand more about addictions, I intend to support Frank as long as he's sincerely working the program, and I see positive changes. He's beginning to show compassion and is doing everything he possibly can to earn my trust.

PART I: GET OFF MY PORCH

Chapter 9

MY RECOVERY PLAN

Today is February 15, 2018. Frank has been gone for three weeks and is doing well in his new home. Things have calmed down substantially, and we're getting along quite well. Communication is easy, and we're able to talk freely about the plans for our own recovery (remember, we can't do it for each other). We avoid talking about past behaviors and events that may trigger each other because what's done is done. We can't move forward if we keep looking back.

Yesterday was Valentine's Day, and it was probably the best one I've ever had with him. Of course he showered me with gifts, which was really nice, but the thing that stood out the most was his demeanor. He was gentle, kind, and relaxed. We played cards, and the conversation was light—he even made dinner, which was delicious. There were some gentle hugs and a few nice kisses. Could it be that he's discovering intimacy? I'm not going to get excited about it because it's too early in the game and I know he's capable of manipulation. But it was a refreshing change.

The first week Frank was gone, he had a hard time adjusting and would find any excuse to come over and hang out. I totally understood but knew I had to start putting a limit on the time he spent here. I was gentle with him and explained that he needed to get used to being alone so we could both work our program without any interruptions. Not to toot my own horn, but asking him to leave was the smartest thing I could have done. Now, he never comes over without asking and respects my need for space.

Frank is an avid reader. Before the separation, I ordered several Brené Brown books to help with my self-esteem and poor body image (I'm a big fan of hers and would recommend any of her books). He knew I was reading one, so I started telling him a little bit about it. I suggested it might be a good read for him to help understand some of my problems. I didn't realize that I already had that particular book in my library, so I gave him the new one. For the next week, he talked daily about what he was learning—not only about me but about himself. Men and women are definitely different and to know those differences can be helpful in understanding each other's needs.

He now has the second book. The first book I gave him was clean, but since I'm normally a huge highlighter, the second book has bright yellow highlights throughout on sections that resonated with me. He's about to get an education about Cat's needs—this could get interesting. The first step of my recovery plan was now in motion. (Highlight, people! You never know when it may come in handy.)

I've set up a daily schedule for my self-care, which is extremely important for my recovery and health. It includes three meals a day, supplements, yoga, cardio, skin care with natural oils, playing the piano, leisure reading, and journaling. I have a page for each day and check things off after I complete them. I find it helpful because before he left, I wasn't eating right, got little exercise, didn't sleep well, and was not using the oils to keep my skin clear. I'll admit I haven't reached the point where I'm checking everything on the list each day, but I'm getting there.

My goal for weight loss is fifteen pounds, and I've already lost six in the last three weeks. It's amazing what you can accomplish when you're not stressed out. I'm sleeping well and don't have to worry about being tense because he's only here when visiting. I started wearing my Fitbit again, and my goal is 5,000 steps a day. I feel good!

Self-affirmations are important for recovery. I got to the point that I didn't have anything positive to say about myself, but I'm going to claim them now. I don't see it as conceit—these are my truths and talents. I'm ready to believe in myself again. Here's my plan:

- I'm going back to piano lessons to finish the course because *I do play well*.

- I'm going to start wearing bright colored clothes because *my body's not so bad*.

- I'll sing when I want to because *I have a good voice*.

- I'll laugh and joke again because *I am a happy person* by nature.

- I'll wear my shorts in the summertime because *I have shapely legs*.

- I'll not compare myself to younger women because *I look pretty good for my age*.

- I'll lose my fifteen pounds because *I want to be healthy* (and look better in my clothes).

- I'll start making jewelry again and doing crafts because *I'm very artistic*.

- I'll read for fun and not education because *I enjoy it*.

- I'll dance in my kitchen if I want to because *I like to dance*.

- I'll spend more time with family and friends because *I'm a social butterfly*.

- I'll not let Frank steal my passion for life because God said *I don't have to*.

So take that, addict! I have more things in mind, but you get the idea. I suggest you make your own list and claim it—it's very good for the soul, and I intend to do each and every one of them. Don't let your partner rob you of who you're meant to be. Take your power back.

My motivation for claiming my truths and talents came from a philodendron. No, I have not lost my mind—it's the truth. I had transferred a plant into a bigger pot, and I think I made it mad. It got all gnarly and started curling up, so being the "plant whisperer" that I am, I did indeed have a conversation with it. Don't laugh—I have a green thumb, and since plants are living things, why not have a chat with them once in a while? I gently explained that it was going to be okay—it just needed room to grow and would be healthy again. After I said that, it hit me— that's what I'm supposed to be doing! I need room to get healthy again and flourish. (About that plant—he's not doing so well yet, but with my help and sweet talk, he'll make it.)

I'm in the early stage of recovery and have shared my plan with you. It's a good one for me and is attainable, but I know it's going to be difficult at times. I don't expect to do it overnight. There will be triggers and emotions that I'll have to deal with, but I must stay on track. I'm sure I'll get frustrated a lot because the addict whipped my tail pretty hard, but with God as my witness I'll take him down!

PART I: GET OFF MY PORCH

Chapter 10

RESTORING INTIMACY

Sexual addiction is an intimacy disorder. Intimacy is the ability to be real with another person (honest, vulnerable, available, and trustworthy). Addicts may have developed the disorder through abuse, abandonment, neglect, lack of nurturing, and many other negative events.

My oldest son and I were having a conversation yesterday about being our authentic selves, and he said something profound. "We've all grown up trying different things to fit in that changes who we are meant to be. Our social life determines our personality, so we're just a bundle of things that seem to work for us." I can absolutely understand how an addiction can become the result of trying to fit in. The addict can become the victim of circumstances, and then the partner becomes the victim of the addict. But once again, the addict made the decisions and is responsible for the consequences. That does not excuse their behavior.

Being the research buff that I am, I wanted to find out more about how couples can regain intimacy after the addict has received treatment and been sober for a good amount of time. This is one of my biggest concerns with Frank. Right now, the thought of him touching me is repulsive because I've been violated, disrespected, and hurt.

The recovery process for the addict involves identifying and acknowledging inappropriate behaviors as a problem and finding sobriety by eliminating those behaviors. The addict also needs to recognize that who they've presented themselves as is based on dishonesty. Addicts need to learn how to be authentically intimate in order to begin the healing process and learn how to have real closeness with others. Recovery is more than daily abstinence...it involves real work. They must discover who they really are, how they were formed, and how they communicate with others.

If they spend real time doing the work earnestly, they can achieve healthy relationships with others. The addict will develop better self-awareness, empathy, understanding for themselves and others, honesty, integrity, and accountability. The intimacy disorder can be healed when the addict understands their self-worth and confidence, which will allow them to risk vulnerability with others. This is the key to true intimacy. They learn to share their truths, feelings of pain, sadness, and ambiguity. A relationship becomes a thing of real value and not something they need to survive or make them feel good about themselves.

This will be a slow process. The addict may be fearful and anxious at times. They need to be honest in their communication and accept themselves with no shame. Once they learn how to have a real closeness with others (authentic intimacy), they can begin to heal.

The addict needs to understand that their betrayal has been traumatic to the partner. They've been hurt by what they didn't know or understand, and if they don't get educated about the addiction, they will continue to get hurt. They are desperately trying to understand what they're up against and attempting to find a way to feel emotionally safe.

When the addict moves deeper into recovery, the partner's sense of emotional safety can be undermined by self-doubt associated with periods of calm as trust starts to grow. When they become aware of a better sense of security and trust, the past may step in to remind them that there were no signs before they were betrayed. Getting hurt again instills fear and doubt. They may go on full alert to protect themselves, and the "emotional rollercoaster" shows up again. Although the addict caused the pain, the wounds are in the partner's heart, and unfortunately they are the only ones who can fix it. The betrayed partner needs to grieve the losses, and the addict needs to support them when they express sadness and pain.

The trauma that resulted from the partner being rejected and mistreated needs to be replaced with new experiences of being loved and cared about. This is the addict's job, which may not be easy but is appropriate because they caused the damage. They need to take responsibility for their unfaithful behavior, admit it was a betrayal of the vulnerability gifted by their partner, validate the excruciating pain of the partner, and express their sorrow for causing that pain.

For the addict, the key to restoring emotional safety with their partner is to tell the truth, and when they do, their words and behaviors will consistently come together. Over time, trust will eventually be restored and they can begin to rebuild the relationship.

Once an addict has accomplished these things and desires a healthy intimate and sexual relationship, they need to ask themselves the following questions:

- Am I maintaining a support group of friends, recovery partners, and sponsor?

- Am I growing more aware of my feelings and talking about them to others?

- Am I reaching out to others when difficult feelings occur?

- Do I desire an intimate relationship out of desperation or to add value to my life?

I've spent a lot of time gathering information about how to restore intimacy after betrayal because Frank and I are going to need it. The biggest job for the addict is to earn back the trust they've destroyed through their destructive behavior. Some of it's a little scary right now for me, so I'm going to start with baby steps. We're only a few months past therapy, but for those of you who are further along in recovery, you might run across something more that helps.

I believe the best thing a betrayed partner can do is *really understand sexual addiction*. Study up and use that knowledge. It won't take away your pain, but it could help with restoring intimacy.

For the addict, it's generally advised to not jump into sexual relationships too soon after therapy. The reason is because the addict already has a lot to concentrate on, and intimacy could throw them off track and back into addiction. Addiction does not happen overnight, nor will the recovery. It may take a long time for the addict to be able to have a relationship, so patience will be necessary.

Married people need a period of adjustment, and it's unrealistic to expect the intimacy to be like it was before because any lost trust needs to be won back. Once the partner has developed certain strategies to deal with the addict's behavior, they will need to abandon those strategies before intimacy can resume. But this will only happen if trust has been regained. Since the addict has lied to you so much, the way you can begin to trust them again is to trust their *actions* instead of their *words*. If persistent difficulties with intimacy become a problem, it would be wise to seek counseling to get past the obstacles.

Make sure you have established effective communication beforehand and are able to discuss any problems that may occur. Encourage the addict because the road to recovery is difficult. Look for the positive in everyday things they do and point them out in a loving manner. Encouragement will fill their emotional tank and help them discover true intimacy. If they stumble, give them grace as well as the truth. God gives us grace when we struggle, so let them know you're on their side.

The addict shouldn't ignore your marriage during recovery. Set a time on a regular basis for date night (preferably once a week), and expect them to act like they're trying to get a second date. Dress up, allow them to open your door, be polite, compliment each other, hold hands, cuddle, and steal kisses—let yourself be wooed!

Don't go to the same old stomping grounds—do something different like a new restaurant or some other place you've never been. Variety is important. It's really impressive if the addict sets the date up by themselves then surprises you. Have fun together, and do something you both enjoy that will relax you and bring out your light-hearted sides. After your date, emotionally connect by talking about your favorite part of the date, what you learned about your partner that you didn't know, and other things you may enjoy doing next time.

Returning to sexual activity won't be easy. The partner needs to give the addict the freedom to be honest if things aren't working right. The addict is going to be nervous because they're afraid of failure. If you insist they finish the job, you risk the chance of them resorting to the old fantasizing habit.

In the initial recovery period, don't "sexy up" with lingerie because you think you have to compete with the pornography he used—that could actually trigger his addiction and interfere with his brain retraining. What he needs to experience is the sexual high which comes from relational and *spiritual* intimacy, not from visual arousal or fantasy. He needs to learn to channel his sexual energy toward you. Take things slowly and allow him to take breaks if he tells you his mind is wandering. It's going to be hard not to take it personally, but it's better if he's allowed to be honest so he can get his heart and head right again.

Once the addict has established sobriety, it will be easier for them to be intimate. Since treatment for sex addicts deals with deep emotions, they can become good partners. Both people need to remember their vows. Are you honoring them? Sometimes renewing the vows can help. You should *never* compare your partner's body to another person. Objectification will make them feel unloved and insecure. If you don't take your marriage or relationship seriously, you *will* become somebody's ex.

The partner needs to set firm boundaries because the addict will take advantage of forgiveness without consequences. Confront them when they step out of line. You'll know the addict is serious about recovery if he's staying in contact with his brothers on the phone daily, reading recovery books, attending group, and confessing to you about being dishonest. Encourage him and give him the confidence to be completely truthful with you. Give each other the right to complain without judgment. You may disagree, but sometimes people just need to be heard. Respect your differences. If you were both the same, one of you would be unnecessary.

Don't make decisions based on emotions because in the heat of an argument it's easy to give up on the marriage. Feelings are unpredictable because they might feel right at the time but be wrong. Never make a fear-based decision because fear is dangerous. Partners who are afraid of getting hurt will make decisions based on fears, not facts. They need to feel safe.

Don't go to bed angry because hurt, resentment, and anger will intensify. Talk it out, even if you have to stay up all night. Submit to each other and be a team. The more committed to the relationship you are, the closer you'll be. Make the decision that you're going to do what's right in God's eyes and act on that decision.

The easiest thing for Frank to say is "I love you," but if he says "I love you *because*..." and tells me *why*, it means so much more and creates a deeper intimacy. If you think of something nice to say about your partner, *say it*. If you think of something to do for your partner, *do it*, and if your partner needs you to change something to feel safe and loved, *change it* (this applies to both people in the relationship).

God's plan for marriage is to become one. Even in the Garden of Eden, there were rules, so if you break the rules, something will die. Be sexually faithful to each other and close your eyes to the sins of the world. Pray for each other—stand up and fight for your relationship. Don't let the sinful acts of the world tear you apart.

In a healthy sexual relationship, people feel safe and connected. Do things to keep the relationship healthy and alive. It may take some time to achieve that goal, but it's worth the patience. *Do the work*, and if the relationship still dies, you know you've done everything you could to save it and can leave without guilt.

Getting help is not weakness—it's wisdom.

Chapter 11

SUMMARY

I *strongly* recommend that the partner of the addict get counseling if they want to heal the relationship and themselves. Personally, I don't believe you'll make it if you don't. Remember, knowledge is power. Even if the relationship has to end, you have been abused, and the pain and memories will follow you into other relationships. If that happens, *you* might become the destroyer and ruin a chance to be truly loved and cherished.

Frank and I attended the same facility, which helped tremendously because the counselors were able to get both sides of the story and personalize our program. Be selective in the therapy you choose—it needs to be comprehensive. I would urge you to make sure your counselor specializes in this addiction. I speak from experience because Frank and I went to several local counselors who only dealt with marital issues. We wasted a lot of money and time and received no help.

I believe therapy for the addict needs to be intensive—not just a weekly visit but an "in-house" program for at least two weeks. Yes, it will cost more, but what's your marriage or relationship worth? Are you willing to make sacrifices for yourself and your loved one to have a healthy relationship? Frank was housed with four other men, and they received individual sessions as well as group. Since they had something in common, it created a more intimate atmosphere. The facility was in the mountains, which created a peaceful surrounding, so they were able to study, relax, appreciate nature, and get closer to God.

Sexual addiction is active now, and it's rapidly destroying the lives of couples everywhere. I personally would consider it an epidemic of huge proportions. We can't just sit back and do nothing when our loved ones have fallen into this destructive addiction.

And above all, the biggest thing you need to do is PRAY! God loves you so much, and He wants only what's best for you and your loved one. If you're comfortable sharing your situation, get some prayer warriors and prayer chains involved. This is an ugly addiction and rarely discussed openly, but as Christians, we need to gather forces and fight. People who fall into this evil trap are looked down on and judged severely. As Christians, we know that the Devil roams the Earth like a roaring lion to kill and destroy, and sexual addiction is becoming easy for him because the secular world is getting filthier every day. Satan is quickly stealing our loved ones, and the children will grow up and be in danger as well.

You may think it was a bit drastic for me to ask Frank to move out. I'm not afraid to take chances now because with everything I've been through, I know I'm in a win-win situation. Yes, he could fail with his recovery, but it's his job to fix it. He could even have an affair. If he does, I've lost absolutely nothing because to stay in a crippled marriage is not my idea of a good and peaceful life. I don't care what it takes—I will be happy and feel safe. "God don't make no junk," and I'm worth every minute that I put into my recovery.

Writing *Get Off My Porch* has helped tremendously with my own recovery. I've spent countless hours researching sexual addiction and the recovery process to provide as much information as possible to help my readers. By doing so, I got quite an education myself. I was ready to throw in the towel and be done with the marriage, but now that I understand how the addict can gain control of an insecure person with a bruised heart like Frank has, I'm willing to give him that last chance.

I've asked God so many times why this has happened to me. I'm a good person, wife, mom, grandma, and friend. I didn't understand until I remembered the Book of Esther (one of my favorites). I now believe it was "for such a time as this."

I intend to get involved, so I am well-educated on this subject. I will give testimony at functions, speak without shame, and comfort those who have been hurt. I may be only one person, but I'm bold and intend to dedicate my life to this cause. It's time for this addiction to be exposed for what it is. I've spent too many years getting knocked down, but now I will stand! My fight will no longer be with my husband but with the addiction.

God commands us to "fear not." I didn't do very well with that, but I'm not afraid anymore. This addiction has been in the closet too long, and it's time to open the door. And when I get to Heaven, I hope to hear, "Well done, my good and faithful servant."

PART I: GET OFF MY PORCH

Chapter 12

A LETTER TO MY LOVE

Dear Frank,

I have faith in you, and I know you can do this. You're a strong man who loves God. But the question is—will you? Please don't love the addict and his sinful ways more than you love God, me, the children, and our beautiful grandchildren. To not have you in the family would be a terrible loss indeed because you are dearly loved.

We've had some horrific moments in our marriage, and I'm not willing to go through them with you anymore. Your decision will be the final say, and you'll have to live with the consequences if you choose the addiction.

If we don't make it, I hope you find what you're looking for. You've always commended me for "staying in the game," but if you can't or won't beat this, that last pitch has been thrown. Remember how we always talked about the wasteland and the chains that bind us? I'd love for you to find that key and bust out of the prison you've put yourself in.

Just remember, no matter what the outcome is I will never stop praying for your recovery and happiness.

I love you,

Cat

PART II

SITTING ON THE PORCH SWING:

NAVIGATING THE DEPTHS OF SEPARATION & PTSD

Chapter 13

OUR NEW BEGINNING

Today's date is March 8, 2018. Frank had therapy early in October of 2017, and I had mine at the end of November 2017. We're fresh out of the chute, but we have some helpful tools to work with. If it appears that it's been easy for us, it certainly hasn't, but we do love each other and believe it's worth a try because nothing else has worked.

This part will now take you through our recovery process. I will include our victories as well as our downfalls and how we handle adverse situations. We have a good education now on the addiction and recovery process but will continue to gather more information along the way. With God's help and our determination, our story may have a happy ending. We're both aware that it won't be easy, but at least we now have hope.

If you're the partner of a sex addict, I can honestly say I understand your pain and frustration. At the risk of sounding like a drama queen, I felt like my heart was literally being ripped apart. You can't identify which emotion to deal with because they're all over the place and you become overwhelmed—it's absolutely devastating. It stays on your mind 24/7, and your peace of mind is shattered.

Let me give you an example: Some days I would feel lonely, fatigued, angry, empty, inadequate, rejected, and helpless, which put me in a not-so-happy mood. I would try to bring myself back around, but lo and behold along came insecurity, anxiety, sensitivity, numbness, and helplessness. It becomes a whirlwind of emotions, so down I went! It's like penny candy—you have a wide variety to choose from, but unfortunately you don't get to choose what you want with adverse emotions—they just show up for free. But you will pay in the end, and the cost may be more than you can afford. It's called depression. That's when everything changes and you're headed for serious trouble. I know because that's what happened to me when my immune system took a big hit and my health was severely compromised.

Looking back, if we would have sought professional counseling from a specialist in sexual addiction sooner I probably wouldn't have gone through the health issues. But in my defense (God knows I need it) we had no idea there *was* an addiction. The only counseling we'd been through was for the marriage—Cat was unhappy but Frank was doing just fine, so it appeared I was the problem.

I'm so glad to be done with the ugly past, so let's move on to my life as a married woman living alone.

Chapter 14

CAT'S IN THE CRADLE

Well, here I am living by myself and enjoying the feeling of safety and loving my time with God. When I go to sleep at night, I imagine I'm cradled in the arms of God and he's watching over me. I'm in charge of setting the atmosphere, and my easy going dog Miss Babette gives me absolutely no problems. She's my "warm fuzzy."

The first day Frank was gone my stress level completely left, and I'm aggressively working my program in between writing this book. I know God is guiding me while I write this because there's no way I could have done it myself in my current condition. My research really helps because I'm learning so much, which keeps me motivated to move forward. I *will* get my self-esteem and health back. No ugly, nasty, disgusting, and controlling addict is going to take me down again. He has to be destroyed in order for me to live. It's time to be a victor instead of a victim.

I believe there are couples who can definitely recover if they use the proper tools and educate themselves. Education is powerful, and you need to learn what you're dealing with. *Honesty and trust must be established in order to recover.* If you've decided there's no hope, you may want to re-think that decision.

My mind was made up, and I had the paperwork in order to file for a divorce before Frank went to treatment. But after I received my therapy, I looked at the situation differently and was willing to give him that absolute last chance (and yes, I still have those documents in a safety deposit box in my name and will be in "go position" if necessary). My biggest concern is that he has full control of how our story will end. He must stay vigilant and always remember the consequences if he chooses the addiction over the marriage.

PART II: SITTING ON THE PORCH SWING

Frank has been gone for over a month now, and we're getting along well. The transition was civil, and things went better than I expected. I refused to help him select a house because it had to be what he wanted and would be comfortable in. We had considered buying a house for rental property before he retired, so if we end up staying together, it will be an extra income. And if we don't, he's all set.

We actually started dating again and are enjoying our time together. He's adjusting to his new home and admitted that the separation was a good idea, although he wasn't happy about it to begin with. He's getting closer to God, got a sponsor for his twelve-step program, is dedicated to his phone meetings five times a week, and rarely misses his webcam meeting with his counselor and the small group he was housed with during therapy. I see a determination in him like I've never seen before.

It appears that Frank's doing a good job, but let me warn you—addicts can be deceiving. We both totally understand this is not going to be a short stint. It's going to take a lot of time and work on his part to earn my trust back. But I have seen some positive changes in him. He speaks softer, smiles more, listens better, shows more compassion for my situation, encourages me with my self-help program, makes sure I have everything I need, and takes me out on dates, among other things.

When he first moved out, he was so afraid of making a mistake because he knows I won't back down this time. He actually had a few panic attacks, which kind of tickled me because now he knows how I felt. I can't even begin to count how many I've had over the years. But lucky for him, I knew breathing techniques to calm him down. He wasn't sleeping well, seemed overwhelmed, and had trouble adjusting. He actually told me he believes God is trying to show him some of the pain I've gone through and said he was sorry. Welcome to my world Frank—God is good!

I believe it's good for him to experience fear for a while because I lived in fear for over eighteen years. It's quite a change from the controlling manipulator I knew. But, I'm always on guard. I don't know this man who's wooing me, and I know better than to get comfortable. Been there, done that, fell down, and got back up too many times. Cat's carrying a big stick right now and won't hesitate to use it!

While Frank is working on his recovery, I'm also working on mine, and it's tough. Despite my past health struggles, I'd like to report that I'm doing much better and know with God's help I will be fine. I discovered the miracle of natural herbs and am vigilant about taking care of myself.

My career as a personal trainer has come in handy too. I just started a mild workout program and am focusing on myself instead of Frank. I'm no longer lying face down with the addict's foot on my back—I've kicked him off and am standing up. The party's over! I'm a child of God and have claimed my right to have joy and peace with or without Frank.

Frank's job is to control the addict and learn to love and enjoy life. But my recovery will be much more difficult because of PTSD. I always thought that was a condition specific to men coming back from war, but I was wrong.

His mere existence made me sick. I'm taking a trip down memory lane here as I type, and I'm not coming up with anything positive to say about how he treated me as a wife, which is sad. He's a good man in many other ways, but he failed miserably in the intimacy, integrity, and respect department.

What's interesting now is that he's exhibiting a lot of good behaviors that would have made a difference in our marriage, but it appears that I wasn't worth it. Ouch! It seems like the old saying "you don't know what you've got till it's gone" may be true. But I don't feel the same way. I knew what I had, and I'm glad it's gone. I didn't have a loving husband—I had a sex addict, and he's not welcome here.

The way I feel right now is typical of the PTSD symptoms I still have to work on. I'm still very sensitive because I *expect* that he's going to say or do something to put me down or hurt my feelings. I'm capable of withdrawing if I feel uncomfortable around him. I tend to relive past events and have intrusive images that put me in a foul mood. I don't have a lot of anxiety when I'm alone, but there are times when I can tell I'm getting anxious around him.

My health problems are still a work in progress and will be the biggest hill to climb. And for the grand finale: mood swings. I can turn on a dime! I'm in his face *right away* if he ticks me off, and I believe this is scary for him (and me too because it's not my nature). I have to admit I've lost control for no reason and had to apologize. I have rage under control but found out that a lot of anger still exists. I suppose he'll have to put up with *me* now, and I don't feel a bit guilty about it. After all, he created this unpredictable creature I've become. The cat claws will sometimes come out, and if he's lucky, they'll retract. I'm definitely a work in progress, and even though it's exhausting sometimes, I will prevail.

Oddly enough, it appears that when I beat one of my bigger symptoms, some of the other ones automatically go away. I've done a lot of self-talk, which has really helped. I tell myself that I'm a good person and have done nothing to damage the marriage. I can say that I was a good wife who treated him well despite the emotional abuse he caused. And most of all, I can now say that I've done everything I can to save the marriage.

Chapter 15

SEPARATION PREPARATION

I named this chapter "Separation Preparation" for a reason. Catchy title, don't you think? I didn't ask Frank to leave for a while this time—I asked him to physically move out. I had to make my recovery all about me and tend to my emotional and physical well-being. This chick was done playing games, and it was high time *for me* to take control now. Near death experiences will change who you are, and I wasn't ready to be dead yet. Frank knows beyond a shadow of a doubt that this is his last chance. I know he loves me dearly because I've seen that side of him, but unfortunately he has to fight his way out because the addict has him cornered. I know he's afraid of losing me, but this has not been a Godly marriage. I can't be a part of it anymore unless he recovers and has control over the addict.

Before he moved out, he agreed to sign two documents I had prepared—a divorce contract (which he signed in the presence of a notary) and a separation agreement. I insisted that he sign the marital home over to me, and he did. When he bought his house, I told him I didn't want to have my name on it, and it isn't. Step one was now complete.

Step two was finances and bills. We amicably split the checking and savings accounts. I already had an account for my jewelry business, so there was no need to open a separate account. (He was not happy back when I opened my own account because he couldn't control it). But both our names were on all the accounts.

Frank has two retirement pensions plus his Social Security, but I only have my Social Security check. We made an agreement to have an automatic deposit into my account from the dividends of our stocks, and the paperwork involved both our signatures so he can't stop anything without my approval. Then we split the bills accordingly. The contract also gives us possession of our individual vehicles. All of this is in the separation agreement and has been signed by both of us and notarized.

Controllers and manipulators often want to be in charge of finances, and Frank was. He's responsible and does a good job. He was also generous with me, and we have a beautiful home and nice vehicles. But once a month, he made it a point to open the checkbook in front of me and announce the difference between last month's balance and the current one. Over time, I got nervous about what I spent and felt like I had to report everything to him. I'm frugal and responsible, but it didn't matter.

When I started receiving my Social Security, he insisted that it be deposited into my account. I knew exactly why he did that—he wanted me to stay out of the main account. That was just fine with me, but it had allowed him to control me.

I need to bring you to the present for a moment. Since Frank doesn't have a computer, he stops by to check his email and have his webcam meeting. We have online banking, and I caught him checking my accounts several times to see what I'm spending and if I'm paying the bills. About a week ago, I told him I wanted him to remove his name from my accounts. He was not happy but complied. He asked why I felt it was necessary, and I softly asked him this question: "Don't you trust me?" He had a deer-in-headlights look that was priceless, and I could barely contain the urge to laugh out loud. He said that he did trust me and still didn't understand why I wanted him to do this. I said he needed to know how it felt to not trust your spouse and worry about what they're doing. After he took his name off, I immediately went to the bank and set up a separate online account for myself with my own password. He no longer asks about my finances.

He did insist that I keep my name on his accounts because he wanted to be accountable for the money he spent. I didn't like the idea at first, but he was adamant about it and told me that part of his recovery is to earn my trust. So, I agreed. I have access to all his finances, but he will not be able to see what Cat's up to. I picked this particular plan because I knew it would be difficult for him to not control me in this area, and it was the best way to show him what it feels like to not trust your partner.

After the first monthly statement we received after the separation, he showed up with every receipt for each transaction in the checking account. He doesn't carry much cash, but he provided receipts for anything he paid cash for. He keeps a running total of his cash at my house and physically shows me what's in his wallet. This was a good idea because in order to get cash, he'd have to withdraw it from his account, which I'd catch. So the boy is really trying.

The divorce contract is more aggressive—fifty-fifty on everything, and there's a lot of "things." He invested well, and we've always maintained a nice savings account. We're not millionaires, but we've lived a comfortable life. I will not touch his retirement checks because he's earned them, so we'll make up the difference in stocks. I *will not* walk away empty-handed because he's the one who put us in this position. I was a good wife, and I'm too old to work full time.

In the event of a divorce, nothing will leave this house except his tools, pictures, and some miscellaneous items because I was generous. I went through every cabinet, closet, and drawers and let him choose what he wanted. I helped him shop for bigger items such as a couch, TV, kitchen dining set, curtains, and vacuum cleaner. I even helped him decorate.

The move was hard for him, and when he was down, I gently reminded him that we can't heal together and this is the only chance to save our marriage. Frank was so kind and cooperative during this process because *I was kind and gentle with him.* If there's Godly love between two people, getting ugly in a situation like this should not be an option. We're both wounded and need to support each other and kick the addict to the curb. I will be there for him so long as he works his program and I see progress. Anything less will be a deal-breaker.

God has made it possible for this easy transition because we have been so blessed with our finances. We believe in tithing and are partners in a children's hospital. We give our time to help those in need and are bold in our faith. He knows Frank's heart and his desire to kick this addiction, and He'll be there for him. But Frank must stay close to God because if he walks away, he's on his own, and that's never a good position for an addict to be in.

Step three was pretty easy. I had to set boundaries. I agreed that he could keep keys to the house in the event of an emergency—like if I was being abducted by aliens (the addict destroyed a lot of things but not my sense of humor, thank God) or if I got sick and needed his help. Occasionally I travel out-of-state to visit relatives, and he agreed to watch Miss Babette and keep an eye on things while I'm gone. He's not allowed to just show up and must call first if he wants to visit. However, he gave me keys to his house and permission to enter unannounced whether he's home or not. Of course, I haven't done that and don't intend to.

As far as intimacy is concerned, he is not welcome to touch me in a sexual manner or approach me about having sex. Our parts work quite well for a couple of old people (we're old but not dead, thank you very much) so while Cat's playground is still open, Frank's been banned from the park. That is not even an option because moving too quickly in that area after treatment could set him back; plus, I'm certainly not yearning for his touch right now.

Hugs are okay as long as he keeps his hands above the waist, and while quick kisses are acceptable, passionate ones are not. So far the only one he's broken is the hug because he thought he'd cop a quick feel, but I foiled his plan and told him he needs to respect my boundaries. He was nice about it and moved his hands back to the green light zone.

Restoring intimacy will be a slow process because we seriously need to get to know each other all over again. The only person I really knew was the addict, and I obviously didn't like him because I wouldn't be sitting here writing a book about sexual addiction.

The last boundary is that I will ask him to leave if an argument starts. I've had to do that twice already because he tried to control or manipulate me. When I called him out on it, he started defending his actions. I've had enough arguing and won't tolerate it anymore. Now, things have been pretty peaceful in that department.

Just a word of caution: I've discovered that as a partner you need to *hold your ground* and be firm with your boundaries in the early stages of recovery. Being gentle and kind when Frank crosses a line works well, but that doesn't mean it will work for everyone. I remind him of our plan for a Godly marriage and ask him what he really wants, and that usually brings him back in line. I could have just slapped his hands away when he touched me inappropriately during the hug and called him a pervert, but that would have been unproductive.

Just remember the brain is affected when there's an addiction, and learning new behaviors is a must for addicts to recover. You can't shame them back to reality because the addiction has become the norm for them. There's been times when I've felt like "sending him to glory" (a saying a dear aunt of mine uses), but I have to keep in mind that he's fragile and afraid of losing me right now, which is not necessarily a bad thing. The prize needs to be in front of him. I will admit that being gentle and kind is difficult for me sometimes because I am also in pain, but I know there's a good man in there. I'm willing to do my part to find him. Yes, the wrath of Cat has come out a few times, but hurt and anger will do that.

PART II: SITTING ON THE PORCH SWING

I want to sincerely compliment Frank for respecting my boundaries. He's doing an excellent job with them now, and he's learning to be humble, kind, and compassionate. I think I'm opening up the softer side of him, and it's beautiful. I just hope he can hang onto it.

God didn't create an addict—he created a man—and there's a good person inside everyone. If you can put your own pain aside and be gentle and helpful, maybe your loved one will realize that's a much nicer path to follow and start acting that way themselves. But the addict must be serious about getting control of their addiction and be diligent about working their program. Try to remember, their pain is real and the road to recovery is tough—just like ours.

Frank has a lot to prove to earn my trust back, and it's not going to be easy for him. I'm learning when to be soft and when to be firm. I make it a point to compliment him on any progress he's making, but I don't give him a pass for any unacceptable behavior. Be careful about the control you give an addict because some of you are probably still vulnerable. I'm doing a good job with vulnerability, but I have to be on my toes at all times.

Remember our reward system with the jar of rocks? He's lost a few here and there, but I'm happy to report that as of this date, he has thirty-nine rocks, each representing a time he was considerate, respectful, and all the things a husband's supposed to be. It's become a game of sorts, but because he's determined to reach his goal of a hundred I absolutely believe it's helping him learn positive behaviors.

I, too, am learning now and starting to feel empowered around Frank. I've been his puppet for so long, and taking my control back feels good. By nature, I'm loving, giving, and loyal. I have good relationships with my family and friends, and those who know me well would describe me as a gentle, loving, and fun person to be around. But the strange thing is, I couldn't be myself around my own husband. It's as if I turned into another person. However, before I went for treatment, I read the books and did the workbook my counselor had recommended to learn about the addiction and how it slowly gains control. I suspected that I had PTSD but didn't want to believe it. I also started doing some research on my own to learn more about what I was dealing with.

When I got out of treatment and came home, Frank had the unfortunate pleasure of meeting his new wife. I was like a cat that had been thrown into a lake—I came out with twenty claws aimed in his direction and was ready to take him down! I had been diagnosed with PTSD, and it wasn't from defending my country— it was from being abused by an addict. I'm trying to come up with a word more powerful than "enraged," and if I ever do, I'm going to ask that it be put in the Merriam-Webster dictionary.

The reality that my own husband had nearly destroyed me was more than I could take. I freely admit that I absolutely hated him that day. However, I was a cool cat that evening and pretended I was glad to see him. I prayed and slept on it, and the next morning I was a different person, even though I didn't know it. I sweetly told him it was time for him to leave. It was obvious he didn't expect it because he couldn't speak for a few seconds. I must have had a look on my face that said, "Don't mess with me buddy," because he quietly said okay. Isn't God good? It's like he blessed me with the courage to stand up for myself, and I'm deeply grateful for that.

There were some pretty tough times before he moved out, but now we both have breathing space to think and get serious about our own recoveries. I was blessed with a wonderful sense of humor and use it in my books, but that doesn't mean it's been all fun and games. Humor lifts me up—just like God does.

Frank came over today, and I could immediately tell that something was wrong. He's been reading a book on narcissism from the partner's point of view, and it really upset him. He had to admit to himself that he was, in fact, a narcissist (which I believe most addicts are). He hates the title and has been in denial, but the truth hit him hard. He started to minimize his condition by telling me about some partners' stories in the book and that there were narcissists much worse than him. He seemed so upset and sad. He said it made him realize how badly he's treated me and how sorry he was.

I wasn't sympathetic and told him directly that it doesn't matter whose story is the worst—he's still a narcissist and emotionally abused me, and I'm the one who has to do damage control. I wouldn't have handled it that way in the past though. I would've felt sorry for him and told him he was a good guy and that it was okay. But now that I'm getting more educated on addictions, I know he's capable of using the sad face and self-persecution to get my sympathy. That's one of the many ways addicts manipulate to get control. I really wish I could believe him this time, but I'm not taking the chance. I don't trust him, and that's going to be the hardest obstacle for us.

Chapter 16

PROVERBS 32

I can't tell you how many years the marriage was good because they were all bad for me. There were some good times here and there but not many. Frank was a happy camper most of the time, and his needs were always met because he had a trained seal for a wife. But my depression got so bad that it kicked the life out of me, and I just went through the motions each day hoping he'd start treating me right. Of course, we did what every dysfunctional married couple does and put on a happy face in public. Needless to say, everyone was shocked to hear about the separation because we appeared to be the perfect couple.

I refused to take antidepressants because I know the negative effects they can cause. I took Valium for two years when I was married to my first husband and got addicted to them. My mind was fuzzy, my reflexes were bad, and I was exhausted most of the time, even though I was only twenty-five years old. We had a toddler, and I worked full time. I drove with that precious cargo in the car for two years while under the influence of a mind-altering drug. I realize now that God's hand of protection had to be on us, and I would like to take this moment to humbly thank him.

I've mentioned several times that I know Frank loves me because I've *seen it* and *felt it*. He's said countless times during our marriage that I'm a Proverbs woman, and he couldn't ask for a better wife (I know, it doesn't make sense to me either, but addicts are complicated individuals). Over the years, he's sent me love letters, written poems, and given me beautiful cards and letters of apology. Although it used to touch me, those feelings went away a long time ago, but once he did something amazing that I'll always remember.

On August 14, 2011 he handed me his creation called "Proverbs 32," which doesn't exist in the Bible because the Book of

PART II: SITTING ON THE PORCH SWING

Proverbs ends at Chapter 31. It is elegantly displayed in the master bedroom and one of my most treasured possessions.

August 14th is not a special date—no anniversary, birthday or anything. He just gave it to me out of the blue. At the time, the marriage was a total disaster, he was deep into his addiction, and I was ill because of my immune system disorder. This was by far the best gift of love he's ever given me, and I'd like to share it with you. (Get your tissues out!)

PROVERBS 32

How beautiful is my Love, Cathy
Her hair is like a field of golden wheat flowing gracefully
in the wind—a symphony of beauty and grace.
Her eyes are like a sea of green reflecting yellow and hazel
from the "Son" and yet able to pierce me to the soul.
Her lips are as soft and sweet as the petal of a red rose
in full bloom.
Her voice is like that of an angel always striving to speak love
and Godly obedience.
Her face radiates with Godliness and is the light of my life.
Her arms are strong from all of her good work and yet warm
and comforting when she holds those she loves.
Her touch is like water to my soul that I crave
and can never get enough.

Her legs are like the branches of a willow—
beautiful and graceful as she moves.
Her skin is like porcelain—smooth to the touch—
clean and white and pure.
Her womanhood is a gift from God—beautiful and alluring
to be only revered and honored.
God has dealt wonderfully with her as she has matured.
She wears the works of her life as a badge of honor—
each one telling a story of her love and grace.
But of all these things that I love, the one I love the most
is her heart, for that is who she truly is.
The love in her heart is as endless as the stars.
The compassion in her heart is as deep as the sea.
The emotion in her heart is like a mighty river.
She is truly one of God's greatest creations.
She is a Godly woman who deserves honor and praise.
I have never been nor will ever be worthy of her love,
but I am blessed beyond measure to be able to say she is my wife.
And when the day comes when she is standing face to face
with God, I know He will say:
"Well done my good and faithful daughter. You have always been
and will always be one of my most beautiful princesses."

Well, that took longer to type than I expected. I had to stop and cry a few times. But I shared it with you for a good reason. You don't know what's in an addict's heart—you only see the ugly behavior that addiction causes. I don't believe they hurt others intentionally, but they're not in control—the addict is. They're trapped in their own Hell, and unless they get some intensive treatment, they will most likely die as an addict. As Frank's wife, I intend to do everything I can to save him and teach him how to love again. I know it will be one of the hardest things I've ever done in my life, but God will be with us.

Ephesians 5:25 says, "Husbands, love your wives, just as Christ loved the church and gave himself up for her..." Frank's got a lot of work to do, but I know so long as he stays connected to God he can do it. Have you ever noticed that God specifically tells men to *love their wives* but doesn't tell women to love their husbands? I have my own opinion about that, but I'll keep it to myself.

Our journey through recovery has just begun. In the following chapters, I'll give you an account of our progress and be totally transparent about situations that arise and how we handle them. We may get lucky and resolve a situation the first time, but I believe most of it will be trial and error. I've dealt with Frank for a long time and have cowered down for the most part. But now that I'm more educated in addictive behaviors, I know some of the things to watch out for. I will continue researching the subject in order to deal with him appropriately, but *I absolutely will not back down*. If I do, he'll gain control again and I'll be back to square one. That's not going to happen.

I'd like to be able to say it's going to be easy, but I'd only be fooling myself. This nice guy that I'm hanging around with right now can be extremely dangerous to my emotional and physical health, and I'm well aware of that. But, I stand firmly on this statement: I SHALL NOT BE MOVED!

Since I've been back from treatment, I pray for all addicts and their partners who have been affected by this horrible disease and ask God to help them recover. I also pray for all counselors whose expertise in this field can save relationships if people would just give them a chance. I'd like to ask you to keep us in your prayers because I'd really like to have a good ending to this story.

Chapter 17

CAT'S BALL OF YARN

PTSD is real. If you have a few of the symptoms you may be able to handle them yourself. But when there are many symptoms that become chronic, I believe you need to seek professional help. Frank's addiction was not the only thing I had to deal with in my adult life, and over time it overwhelmed me until everything became a tangled mess.

As I've already mentioned, I was married before. During the marriage, I had to deal with a huge amount of stress. I'm not going to go into detail because my ex-husband and his wife are good friends of ours now, and I won't throw him under the bus. We were married for seven and a half years, divorced for three, and then remarried for fourteen more years. We tried marriage counseling but just weren't able to keep it together.

During the time my ex and I were married, my brother Dave, who was my absolute best friend, was injured in a plane crash. He wasn't expected to live, so my mother and I flew out the next day after receiving the news. He miraculously pulled through and eventually went home with twenty-four-hour nursing. His feet had been crushed, his thumb was torn off, and he had massive head injuries. He wasn't able to speak or walk and didn't seem to understand much. He lived out-of-state, but I was able to visit him almost every month.

Dave was making huge progress and was being rehabilitated. He was able to understand conversations, use the remote control, feed himself, and drink from a glass. In therapy, they were using a board stand, and he was gaining strength in his legs. The therapists gave us a lot of hope, and we were elated. I don't believe I've ever prayed so much for anyone in my life, and it was obvious God was answering those prayers.

But his recovery took an ugly turn. His wife had gotten pregnant with one of his friends and continued on with her life while paying little attention to Dave. She lived in an elegant manor (which was obtained by a work comp settlement because he was on assignment when the plane crashed), and Dave was housed in the old servant's quarters by the driveway. Dave was a nationally well-known photojournalist, and they had always lived a comfortable life. I will say he had everything he needed to recover...except love.

After about ten years, the nurses started telling us that she was abusing him—both physically and emotionally. She became arrogant around us and treated us like we were beneath her. We knew if we confronted her that she would take away our visiting privileges, so our hands were tied. After Frank and I were married, he went with me, and we always prayed over Dave. I remember one time in particular that I told him God is watching over him, and he smiled. To this day, I can still see that beautiful smile.

In the latter months of 2004, my mother and step dad went to visit him. We got a hysterical phone call from my mom. She said his wife had prepared a form and wanted my mom's signature agreeing to take away Dave's medication and food so he could die because he had no quality of life. She had also taken him out of therapy and fired most of his caretakers.

Frank and I drove down the next day. We asked her to let us have Dave and we'd take care of all his needs, but she said absolutely not. She had previously told us that she'd only received one-half of the settlement and would get the rest if he died. I obtained a lawyer in the state they lived in and fought for months, but it was no use. Dave died on May 24, 2005, and my best friend was gone. The only good news is that she shipped his body home. The cemetery is right down the road from us, and he's buried next to my dad.

PART II: SITTING ON THE PORCH SWING

My dad was a wonderful man with a contagious sense of humor. I come from a family of seven and have two brothers and two sisters. Dad provided a good living, and we had everything we needed. We weren't rich, but there was a whole lot of love. He taught us good values and always had time to play some Yahtzee or listen to our problems. I don't care what it was—Dad always had the answer and knew the Bible like the back of his hand. He didn't push religion on us, but we certainly knew the dos and don'ts of life. To me, he was the perfect father.

Dad died on February 19, 1998, eight months before Frank and I were married. He was only seventy years old. I so desperately wanted him to walk me down the aisle again. I was really upset, but my son from Colorado surprised me and drove all night to Illinois to do the honor. Our family had always been close, and we all loved each other dearly. Dad had been battling congestive heart failure and had gone through two open-heart surgeries, but he just couldn't hang on. I miss him terribly.

My mother was a loving parent too, but she changed about ten years ago. My baby sister and I have always been close as adults, but as we grew older, it appeared that mom was jealous of our relationship. We're not sure if that's the problem, but she always complained that my sister didn't pay much attention to her. However, my sister works a lot of hours and doesn't live in the same town. She would get angry when my sister and I spent time together, and it became apparent that she wanted to destroy our relationship.

She lied vehemently to each of us about the other and caused a separation. She also lied to my other sister and brother, and they turned on me as well. But, we were able to patch things up within a year or so. Mom and I had reconciled and things were going well. She never apologized but made me believe my little sister was the problem. My sister and I didn't speak for seven years, and when we did, the truth came out.

I'm happy to report that my sister and I have gotten back together and have been making up for lost time. Mom pretended she was happy about it, but she wasn't done with us yet. Last fall, she lied about me again by attacking my character to people outside of the family. Then she went after my sister again with lies—but my sister stood up for me and fought back. Now I know who really loves me, and I'll let nothing come between my beautiful sister and me again.

Now my mom's driven away two daughters, but she said, "I still have two children, and that's just fine with me." I can't imagine losing one of my children, let alone driving them away! She's been tested for Alzheimer's and her mind is perfectly fine, so we can't use that excuse.

After Dad died, Mom married a good man who's stable financially and treats us like his own. He took her on numerous trips overseas and showered her with jewelry and anything else she wanted. Over the years, my mom became arrogant, manipulative, and controlling. It appears that love of money has become more important than anything—even her children. She's also turned her husband against his own children and convinced him to change his will. She forgets where she came from, and it breaks my heart.

Between Frank's addiction, his daughter and ex-wife's behavior, the divorce from my first husband, my brother and father's deaths, my mother's abuse, and my health issues, you can see how these things have taken a toll on my emotional and physical well-being. I don't believe there's anything more painful than being hurt and betrayed by a family member, especially a parent. She's either forgotten or doesn't care that all five of her children have always loved and respected her.

Some of you may be experiencing multiple problems, which will definitely add to your stress level, and that can become dangerous. I've been abused by two of the most important people in my life—my husband and my mother. But God has been gentle with me, and I've learned that it's okay to separate yourself from people who steal your peace and joy. You can't control them—you can only control yourself.

Now, I'm going to move forward and stop *allowing* my mother to interfere with my emotions and progress in trying to heal our marriage. I didn't ask to be her daughter, but I can walk away from her abuse. God has given me peace about that. I pray for her every night and ask God to heal her cold heart because there's nothing I can do without getting hurt again.

Chapter 18

SHAME AND BLAME

When a couple is dealing with addiction, shame and blame play a huge part in the relationship. But until the addict gets professional help, the shame and blame could fall on the partner of the addict.

When I first discovered Frank was into objectifying women and pornography, I confronted him when I witnessed his inappropriate behavior. Every time he denied it and blamed it on my insecurity and imagination. It was particularly difficult for me while I was going through menopause because he used that against me.

He played the menopause card with his daughter and ex-wife. He never stood up for me when they misbehaved and blamed it on menopause, so I didn't have a chance. We went through menopause quite easily because when I knew I was having an emotional day, I'd let him know.

Over the years, I started to believe I was the problem, so I became *ashamed* of my behavior and accusations towards him. There were times when I apologized to him to keep the peace when I knew I was right. Then, I started taking the *blame* for our marital problems.

In *Get Off My Porch*, I briefly describe gaslighting, but now I'm going to go into more detail because I believe it's extremely important for a partner to know how and why the addict uses this tactic. I know this information is going to help me tremendously with my own recovery because it's the very thing that caused my emotional and physical problems.

Again, gaslighting occurs when someone attempts and eventually succeeds in convincing you that your feelings, thoughts, or perceptions of reality are not true. They use manipulation and intimidation to make you doubt yourself. Here are some of the signs that indicate gaslighting may be happening to you:

- You find yourself apologizing to the addict when it's not your fault.

- You ask yourself if you're oversensitive.

- You avoid the addict to risk being put-down or intimidated.

- You feel like you're a different person and don't feel as confident as you used to.

- You make excuses for the addict's behavior.

- You have trouble making decisions and second-guess yourself.

- You experience confusion.

- You avoid certain topics in conversation with the addict.

- You try to be perfect and get anxious if you think you've done something wrong.

- You don't understand why you can't be happy even though there are good things in your life.

- You become self-conscious about your body.

- You start to believe they don't love you and feel like you're being used.

I felt all of the above, plus a whole lot more. At one point, I thought I was going crazy and actually started hating myself. Through research and prayer, these are some of the strategies I discovered to combat my emotions:

- If I feel out of control, I tell myself I'm a good person and *will* recover.

- I confirm this was not my fault and I was a victim.

- I realize my feelings are valid and I don't need to justify them.

- If there's a power-struggle with Frank, I shut it down and take a break.

- I remind myself that God loves me unconditionally.

- I tell myself I'm getting healthier every day.

- I remind myself that I have a good support group who will always be there for me.

Since we all have different situations regarding the addict, I suggest you come up with a list of your own that applies, write them out, and read it daily.

Betrayal trauma is a terrible thing. It can get so bad that it becomes emotional abuse (which is what I experienced) and can turn your life upside-down. I blamed myself for so many things and felt ashamed. You can lose touch with reality and end up living a miserable, unfulfilled life.

On a brighter side, I'm finding out that shame and blame has a way of turning itself around. Frank appears to be doing well with his recovery so far, but he's starting to feel ashamed and is blaming himself for the destruction of our marriage. *I absolutely allow him to own it and I confirm it!* I give him zero slack and don't water things down to make him feel better, but I also commend him on his new-found knowledge because he's discovered the truth.

If he wants to beat himself up emotionally, that's just fine with me because he's beginning to experience some of the pain I've gone through. However, hanging on to shame and blame too long is not a good thing because it can lead to depression. I've given him a few self-help books that I've been using for myself. I have to admit though there's still a part of me that wants him punished, and that little voice in my head says, *Why should I help him at all?* But I don't think God would be too happy with me, so I play nice when I can. I know my stinking thinking is based around the addict and have to remind myself that I'm looking for the good and trying to eliminate the bad.

I suppose it's time for an update on our progress so far. Things have been surprisingly calm, and we're getting along very well. We've had a few bumps in the road but were able to work through them. We stay in contact daily either by phone or spending time together but not all day. We sleep in our own homes, and there is no sexual activity—just a hug or kiss from time to time.

Frank is doing an excellent job respecting my boundaries. If we're together and I say I'm getting a little anxious, he leaves. We go on dates and sometimes do our weekly shopping together. We've been to antique and resale shops, and he was the one who suggested it, which meant a whole lot to me because he never cared for that activity. Actually, he's beginning to enjoy it too.

He calls every night before he goes to sleep, and we go through an exercise the counselors call "FANOS." We openly discuss our feelings ("F") whether they're good or bad and talk about it. We give positive affirmations ("A") about ourselves. We express any needs ("N") we may have. And we own ("O") positive or negative things about ourselves. We do not do the "S," which stands for sobriety, because he has his own sponsor. I don't want to know if he's had a setback because it may trigger me.

We're beginning to set a new normal, and he's working hard to earn my respect and trust. But it's going to take time, and he understands that. It's not going to be easy because there's nineteen years to undo, but so far things are positive. However, I keep my guard up because I know from experience that addicts can put on quite a show, and I'm not even close to trusting him yet.

PART II: SITTING ON THE PORCH SWING

Chapter 19

EMOTIONAL ROLLER-COASTER

Being blessed to have the luxury of living apart has been a Godsend for me. Frank and I are equally yoked when it comes to being frugal with our money and invested wisely. I'm grateful because there's no way I would have stayed with him if we had to live under the same roof. Going to one's "own corner" to decompress isn't easy when you're living together.

I was so miserable for over eighteen years and couldn't figure out why God didn't do something to alleviate my pain. I kept asking him, "Why is this happening to me?" I'm a good person and didn't deserve to be abused this way. My immune system was shot, and I was so weak and sick. But amazing as He is, I'm still here and getting healthier every day. I believe I've figured out what it's all about.

I know how much you hurt and I sincerely want to help. I've learned by trial and error, and if I can say even one small thing to help you, then I need to do it.

Sometimes we find ourselves in the "wasteland." It's a miserable place to be, but that's where we learn how to deal with adverse situations. I think the class God chose for me was "Courage 101." I allowed the addict to beat me down to a pitiful mass of nothing, and I'd given up.

Negative emotions can be dangerous if left unattended. They can affect your peace of mind, self-worth, body image, common sense, etc. They can literally change who you are. Even everyday chores became difficult for me because I either felt bad or couldn't stay focused. It's a terrible place to be, and over time, you just don't care about much of anything.

Cat was crawling around dragging through life, but good ole Frank was stepping over me so he wouldn't be inconvenienced in his quest to be a disgusting sex addict. I have a nice wardrobe, but my color of choice around him was black—that way, I could hide my imperfections. When I think about that now, it's like I was in mourning for our dead marriage.

I started writing *Get Off My Porch* before Frank moved out. There were many times I got upset because I was reliving some bad episodes in the marriage, and his presence was a constant reminder. I was just typing away and minding my own business one day when I realized why God had allowed me to go through such pain. I love the book of Ester and have taught it in women's groups. The quote "for such a time as this" hit me like a ton of bricks.

I realized I had to go through the wasteland so I could write my books to help others. It was hard at first to be so vulnerable and tell my story because I was embarrassed and depressed. But now it's getting much easier. It's actually helping me too because I'm gathering knowledge through research.

Even though we're apart, negative emotions and images of what he's done still attack me because of the PTSD. I mentioned earlier that we've hit a few bumps in the road, but last week the "you-know-what" hit the fan. This one was a sinkhole!

Things had been going well until I asked Frank if he wanted to read what I had in this book so far since he'd shown an interest. He said sure, but four days later I asked if he'd read it and he said no because he was reading something else. That hit a nerve because I'd been working almost every day on this book and dealing with bad memories. He'd read a little bit of *Get Off My Porch* and said it was "too emotional" for him. Seriously? *He* was the one that caused all the pain I've been writing about!

I'm *way* past angry today. My PTSD is running on all cylinders, and I've been having flashbacks for two days. I'm blaming him for everything except World War II right now. I've cut off contact with him except for a few texts or phone calls. I took

PART II: SITTING ON THE PORCH SWING

our dog to his house to spend the night and couldn't wait to pull out of that driveway!

Even though I've become pretty educated on PTSD, it hits me with no warning. I have now placed him in the "selfish, arrogant, narcissistic, controlling, and manipulative basket" and slammed the lid.

The day after Cat had her "hissy fit," I told him he needed to learn more about PTSD to understand what I'm going through because I had taken the initiative to learn about his addiction. He agreed, so I gave him the book *Your Sexually Addicted Spouse* by Barbara Steffens and Marsha Means, which I would highly recommend to any partner of a sex addict. It's a hard read, but you'll learn so much about your pain and how to deal with it (and your significant other should read it, too.)

After Frank came back from treatment, he read the book, but he was so involved with his own recovery that he didn't absorb much. But this time he's reading it thoroughly to understand what causes PTSD and the damage it can do both mentally and physically to the partner of the addict. He was upset after the first chapter and felt guilty about what he's done, but he hasn't seen anything yet—wait till he gets to the third chapter!

This is day two of Cat's stand-off with Frank. We've been texting back and forth this afternoon because I don't even want to hear his voice. Sometimes I get so overwhelmed and angry about how bad this situation is that I can hardly handle it. This is one of those times, and he's aware of it.

I'd like to change the topic because I just received a text from Frank that I'd like to share. He's learning to be more compassionate, and he sent me his daily meditation.

I will never leave you or forsake you. When no one seems to understand you, simply draw closer to me. Rejoice in the one who understands you completely and loves you perfectly. As I fill you with my love, you become a reservoir of love overflowing.

I truly love God, and I know He's always there for me. I really needed that. I don't believe I've ever gotten as close to God as I am now. When I heard the words "sex addict," my whole world changed and I fell apart. My anger turned into rage, and God waited. Then my pity party lasted about two months, and God waited. My rage turned into hatred, and God waited. Finally, I reached out, and God embraced me.

I know God's with me and understands what I'm going through, but I need to learn how to combat PTSD because it's difficult. Once again, God will wait while I learn, but He won't let me hit bottom this time unless I choose to. Yes, I'm still upset with Frank because he was being selfish and didn't support me on something I'm passionate about. But I've had a setback and am once again dealing with damage control.

I'm sure you know by now that addicts are extremely selfish. I need to hold my own and try to teach Frank the pecking order— God first, then yours truly second. Not Frank *first*, then what Frank wants *second*, then what Frank needs *third*, then God (in case of an emergency), and then *maybe* wife, kids, grandkids, and friends unless something more important to *him* pops up. If he doesn't put God first and me second, he'll never win this fight with the addict. I know Frank truly loves God, but he's allowed the addiction to get in the way of serving Him.

Getting back to our current situation, since Frank moved out, the focus has been mostly on him because I was rolling along just fine. I was doing my job of encouraging him and complimenting him on his progress. He didn't have a job to do with me because he said I've been calm and he's enjoyed my company.

But PTSD can be fickle. It's on you before you know it, and you lose control. Your emotions can turn on a dime, and you can't think rationally. A lot of the PTSD symptoms I previously listed, which I *thought* went away after Frank moved out, are back. Writing these books has been the biggest achievement of my life because I know God is using me as an example to help the victims of sexual abuse, and I am honored.

Frank's nonchalant attitude about reading my books as I write them really hurts. I've seen some good changes in him and thought he would be my biggest cheerleader, but I was wrong. He was the one who said I was being too easy on him when he read a small portion of *Get off My Porch*. I was trying to protect him so he wouldn't look so bad, but he said I needed to be totally transparent.

However, I do believe if I was writing a book about how it feels to be married to the perfect man, he would have been reading over my shoulder and telling me what to write. It's always been about him, and I was just along for the ride until we crashed.

I think the Devil must have created PTSD because it's ugly, dark, and can be very destructive. It's difficult to separate the sex addict from the real person because it's not an addiction you can *see* like alcoholism or drugs. It's hard to trust Frank because I don't know which one I'm dealing with at the time.

Please be warned—*PTSD is a real medical condition*. I know because I'm living with it. It's not reserved for soldiers in the military. The addict has stolen my joy, peace of mind, and health. Don't hesitate to get professional help like we did because the consequences could be devastating. But what I do know for sure is *I will get through this with God's help.*

I have to be the selfish one now, and Frank will just have to wait until I get over this mountain. He appears to be upset about being the source of my setback, but that's okay because I've been upset for a long time and maybe it's his turn in the barrel.

Chapter 20

WAITING TO POUNCE

I'm beginning to relax and enjoy my freedom. The struggle with PTSD continues, and my symptoms appear to escalate when I'm around Frank. As much as I hate to admit it, I believe I'm actually waiting for him to make the smallest mistake so then I can pounce on him. He's being sweet and loving, has a whole lot of patience, and is there for absolutely anything I need.

He's walking on eggshells right now when he's around me, but I don't seem to be able to stop myself. Sometimes when everything's going well, I look at him and remember the sacrifices I made to hold the marriage together and the health issues his behavior has caused, and I get angry all over again. His job is to stay sober, tell the truth, and stop the control and manipulation.

My recovery is much more complicated. I need to feel safe and learn how to manage my own life again because I allowed him to control my emotions. I have to retrain my brain and start believing in myself again. This involves a lot of self-talk, which is difficult, but I'm doing pretty well so far. I'm not there yet, but I'm a work in progress and understand that it's going to take time. Nineteen years of brainwashing is hard to undo.

The addict made me believe I wasn't worthy of being loved sexually because I don't have the body of a twenty-year-old anymore. I made the horrible mistake of comparing myself to the younger women he was objectifying, and my self-image suffered tremendously. I felt like a fat, old, worn-out cow and scolded myself daily.

Unfortunately, partners of sex addicts almost always end up comparing themselves to the addict's choice of fantasy. I knew I could never look like that and told him so many times, *but an addict will not care about your pain.* They may feel guilty for a short time, especially if you're visibly upset, but it doesn't last because they have been programmed through addiction to cope with their own pain.

Comparing myself to others took me down a dark and painful road. It got to the point that *every time* I got dressed for the day it ended up being an emotional disaster. I'd try on many ensembles to find something to cover up what I considered my imperfections, hoping he'd find me attractive. Crying was almost always involved. Some days I would talk myself into not caring what he thought and put on some colors—but I always changed my mind and wore black.

My self-talk was sinful to say the least. Some of the dialogue I used was, "What's wrong with you?""Look at that fat," "No wonder he doesn't want you," "You're too old to wear yellow or pink," "Cover that nasty stuff up," "Why do you even try?" "You don't deserve to eat," and "No wonder he looks at other women."

Here's my truth now—I was only twenty-five pounds overweight because of the Prednisone, but I saw myself as an obese and disgusting woman. Right now, I'm only fifteen pounds over my goal, and I'm proud of myself! I've never been an emotional eater, so food wasn't the problem—stress was. It slows down the metabolism, and even though I knew this as a retired personal trainer, I chose the absolute worst route to take. I stopped eating except for one meal a day, which made things worse. I convinced myself that I didn't deserve to eat.

The personal trainer in me could advise you to not compare yourself to others, exercise daily, eat right, avoid stress, think good thoughts, tell yourself that you're beautiful and worthy of being loved, don't let his behavior affect you, and lots of other things at which point you'd probably throw this book in the trash. But even though I'm educated in this field, I couldn't help myself. All I can do is share what I'm learning and actively doing that's helping me.

But let me tell you right now, *the emotions and pain you're going through are real.* They're the result of the abuse you've suffered from their addiction. You haven't been dealing with your husband or significant other—you've been fighting an invisible evil that has manifested in their brain due to their lack of ability to handle their own pain. *This does not excuse their behavior—they have to own what they've done to you.* But once they have received treatment, it *does* become their fault if they don't follow the recovery program and show progress.

The biggest obstacle for me right now is triggers. These involve past events that pop in my head uninvited—lies he's told to cover his addiction, putting the blame on me because he had me convinced I was insecure, watching him objectify women and ignore my intimate needs, his manipulation, and the control he had over me. He made me feel like an ignorant child.

As people develop a loving relationship, a close bond occurs. They begin to trust each other and have a sense of safety. They look forward to spending time together and miss each other when they're apart. Love and compassion for each other becomes the norm. However, when couples are *extremely* close, the pain of betrayal is much worse.

Frank and I developed a good friendship before we started dating, and I totally trusted him. But after we were married, everything changed. Frank left, and the addict took his place. He'd won the prize, and the deception started. Little by little, year after year, he reprogrammed me. He knew just when to back up and be kind and loving. He could turn on the tears in a heartbeat, and I'd feel guilty for being upset. He took advantage of my devoted love for him.

I've always been a fun-loving person with a lot of patience and compassion. No matter what he did, I always forgave him. But about ten years ago, I started fighting back (not physically—I'm messed up but not stupid, and he's never been physically abusive). I called him out on every inappropriate incident, and he'd lie, manipulate, and argue (standing up and talking down to me in the alpha pose of course), refusing to back down until I emotionally caved in.

We played this game for many years, and over time, I started having panic attacks and my body reacted to the stress. That was a huge red flag I missed, but I was determined to convince him that I wasn't the problem. Two years ago, I gave up and just went through the motions of being a wife and was too tired and sick to fight. The addict had won.

We're getting along okay now, but I'm so guarded all the time. In therapy, I discovered that I was suffering from abandonment, which can happen in an intimate relationship when our loved one betrays our trust. It can cause betrayal trauma, which can become critical and cause emotional and physical stress. At that point, the relationship can be dangerous because everything you believed was a lie, and the addict has to regain your trust.

Until I went for treatment, I was fighting a losing battle. Every time I started feeling better, he'd act out and start the manipulation and lie all over again. I never had enough time to get over the last incident before he betrayed me again, so his behavior constantly interrupted my healing. That's why Cat now has PTSD.

Now, part of the healing depends on processing my pain. I couldn't figure out how to do that because there was so much to deal with and I was overwhelmed. But thanks to research, I discovered that one of the biggest steps you can take is to tell your story, and I'm so into it that I'm writing books for the whole world to see! Total vulnerability feels good. I know now that I was the victim of a sex addict, it wasn't my fault, and I have absolutely no shame about it.

I realize I may be judged by some of my readers for staying in such a crippled marriage. But, I think there are those who will applaud me for the courage to get an education so I can understand how my husband got pulled into such a horrible addiction. I believe that *no one chooses to be an addict—*

circumstances in life can take a person down so hard that they begin looking for ways to relieve the pain, and Frank definitely had a lot of trauma in his life before I met him.

As you can tell, I take my marital vows very seriously—especially the *"in sickness and in health"* part. My husband is *sick* with an addiction, but he can beat it if he uses the tools and knowledge he's received. I have *health* issues, but I'm being proactive and getting better all the time. But the best news is that God's doing a work for both of us, and if we're in him, who can be against us? And look at me—he's even chosen me to write books to get the word out and help others. I'm so blessed it's getting ridiculous, but my mind is still messy. They say that's normal with PTSD, but it's bringing me down pretty hard right now because I have a bad attitude.

I'm still like a cat ready to pounce on a defenseless mouse. I've confessed this to Frank, and he now understands more about what I'm going through because he took my advice and read up on PTSD. So now I guess he needs to be on guard (that felt so good to say!). I'm not proud of my behavior, but I have to work through it since it's my reality. I'm fighting flashbacks daily, which makes me very angry, so we're not spending much time together.

I still have a hard time accepting the fact that I have PTSD. It's an awful disorder, and you never know when it's going to hit. It's like a rerun of a bad movie with no pause or off button. I'm trying desperately to find some type of distraction to drive it away, but I'm not good at it yet.

My first attempt was to play the piano, but I felt like a beginner because I couldn't focus (even though I'm headed for the masters). My next one was shopping, but that just made me mad because I couldn't find anything to buy. Reading just for pleasure is a waste of time because I don't absorb much. When I research I'm absolutely focused, but that's a tedious job with a lot of triggers because of the subject matter.

The last two attempts I made might help, but I'm having a hard time getting started each time. I make bracelets for the local cancer center, so I've made about sixty of those so far. It's taken me several weeks when I normally can make a hundred a week. I love to paint statues and found one for my sister's seventieth birthday, but I've only painted on it for about two hours. Thank God her birthday is not until November!

Please don't stay in the game too long before getting help. I know I've warned you a lot, but you have no idea of the consequences you may suffer. I do. It's not worth your health or peace of mind. I pray a lot for the partners and addicts as I'm writing my books, and I pray right now that you'll gain wisdom from my experience and be smarter than I was.

Chapter 21

CAT'S PTSD RECOVERY PLAN

I've been frustrated for some time now and am finding it difficult to move forward with the relationship. Frank and I are still getting along, but I'm starting to feel like he's just a friend. We enjoy spending time together, but I don't think I'm in love with him anymore, which saddens me. I need to be careful right now because depression could be lurking just around the corner!

I've been trying to recapture the love I had for him, but I can't seem to get it back. Maybe I'm going through a trust issue or subconsciously expect him to fail because he's never kept his word about stopping the destructive behavior that destroyed our marriage. It could also be the fear of getting hurt again, which could affect the health progress I've made.

I've talked a lot about PTSD and have been doing more research on how to control it. I recently realized I was only using occasional distractions when I needed to clear my mind, and it wasn't doing much good. But I've found some really good tools I believe can help, and I'd like to share them.

When we make the decision to take action, we gain power, which makes us feel hopeful instead of helpless. Response to trauma is normal with PTSD, and recovery is a daily process. Healing doesn't mean you'll forget the trauma or won't feel pain when thinking about it, but you may have fewer symptoms and manage your feelings better.

I think the most important thing you can do is get an education on what PTSD really is. You can't fight something if you don't know what you're dealing with. If you learn about it, you'll realize that you're not alone or going crazy—it's not an uncommon or rare condition. I've decided to use the following techniques for my recovery, and maybe it will help you too.

Find ways to relax your body, which can also help clear your mind. The things I'm going to start doing are stretching my body with yoga, listening to my favorite music and singing along, spending time outside and enjoying nature, doing deep breathing exercises, and my all-time favorite: praying and including all the things I'm grateful for. I've made a list of all the bad things in my life, which ended up being much shorter than the list I made of the things I'm grateful for. Figure out what relaxes you and really make an effort to do it, but make sure they're positive activities.

If you're creative, get back to those arts and crafts. Finish a project and pat yourself on the back for a job well done. It's okay to be proud of yourself. I'm back to making my bracelets and painting the statue for my sister. I haven't played the piano yet, but I will as soon as my mind clears up a bit.

Remind yourself that bad thoughts are just memories, which are natural to have when you've been traumatized. Maybe you can talk to someone you trust about it. But keep in mind, they will lessen with time. If you have nightmares and wake up in a panic (I've done that one a lot), realize you're reacting to a dream and that there is no current danger. You may need to get up and walk around to regroup before trying to go back to sleep.

If you have difficulty falling asleep, try to keep a regulated sleeping schedule and avoid a lot of activity a few hours before retiring. Avoid caffeine, which definitely affects your sleep. If you're in bed and start worrying or having bad thoughts, get up and do something pleasant like reading a good book (be selective—there may be triggers) or drinking some warm milk, herbal tea, or whatever you find enjoyable to calm your mind.

If you get angry, take a time-out and walk away if necessary. Being angry is detrimental to your well-being because it increases your stress level and can cause health problems (boy, do I know *that* one).

If you have difficulty staying focused, *slow down* and give yourself a break. Don't overload yourself with tasks—spread them out if necessary. Also, depression can interfere with your concentration, so keep an eye on that.

If you have trouble expressing positive emotions, remember this is a common reaction to trauma, so don't feel bad about something you can't control at that moment.

Think back to something you used to enjoy, step away from your pain, and do it. You may not feel like it, but once you get going you may be surprised how it can lift your spirits.

Do something nice for someone. That's a big one for me, and I've always expressed my love for the people I care about through small things like telling them how special they are to me or crafting something and giving it to them for no special reason—just to show my love.

It's difficult to get back into your life when you have PTSD. It's not productive to isolate yourself (although it's a common reaction) and avoid people. It will be difficult at first, but get back to your regular routine as soon as possible. Also, self-care is extremely important. You need to exercise, eat right, and get a lot of rest. If you don't, your anxiety could get worse, and that could lead to depression.

I hope these tips help you. I just started doing some of them, so I can't tell you how it's working for me yet. I know it's unrealistic to do all the enjoyable things I listed every day, but my plan right now is to just pick one or two.

Partners of any type of addiction used to automatically be labeled as "co-dependent," but they've found out that's not always the case. I certainly didn't fit into that category, and I'm grateful for that discovery because I wouldn't have received the proper help I needed to get over my trauma.

If you keep remembering circumstances and the pain they caused, there's a chance you will actually *experience* the trauma and pain over and over again. But you're meant to go through them only when they occur. I'm learning to grab those memories when they pop up. In my mind I imagine a large shredder, and I destroy them. I haven't mastered it yet, but it seems to be working for me. Don't make it harder than it needs to be—they're just bad memories that steal your joy.

I'm tired of moping around like I've lost my best friend. I'm going to have some fun doing what I enjoy because I know it will help with my self-esteem and health. And above everything else, I'm going to *laugh and smile* more.

Chapter 22

SUMMARY

I sincerely hope that the information I have provided in *Sitting on the Porch Swing* will help with your recovery. I urge you to personalize your program according to your circumstances and be kind and loving to yourself. This is not a life sentence—you will survive, but there's work to be done.

If you've already made the decision to end the relationship with the addict, I believe you should still do this for yourself because the pain you've suffered and the trust that's been broken could affect future relationships. You deserve to be loved and respected. Remember, you did not ask for this and it's not your fault, but unfortunately you have to undo the damage their addiction caused. To me, it's been a learning experience, and if our marriage has to end, I'll know what to watch for if I have to start over. Education is powerful.

Before I finish *Sitting on the Porch Swing*, I'd like to give you a progress report. As far as I can tell, Frank's still diligently working on his program. He's submitting an outline to a local pastor for approval so he can speak to a men's group about addiction. He's eager to share his knowledge to help others, which is a good sign because he'll have to tell his story—which isn't easy (I can certainly relate to that). Since I'm used to a selfish narcissist, I'm impressed with this move.

I received a call three days ago from the wife of a couple dear to us. She was devastated because she found out her husband had been looking at inappropriate material on the computer. They knew about our situation, so she was reaching out. Of course, I immediately tapped in to help her because she's aware of the knowledge I've received from counseling and research.

She asked Frank if he could help by talking to her husband, and he readily agreed. He's made himself available, and the husband is opening up and asking for help. This was a pretty big deal to me because Frank is using his knowledge to help others. He has two projects now with the church and the husband, which is a good thing because it keeps him focused on the tools he uses for his own recovery.

I can definitely see a difference in his demeanor, and he's been more patient and kind for about two weeks solid. He seems focused on my needs and is doing everything he can to earn back my trust. I'm starting to let him know that I'm proud of him, which gives him motivation.

Unfortunately, his report card looks much better than mine. I'm like a seesaw that occasionally gets stuck in the down position, and I stay there until I can work through negative emotions. I'm not good at staying steady, but I'm getting better. I'm aware it's all about fear. I'm waiting for that bully on the playground to knock me down, so I retreat to my safe space and hide.

I understand this is normal with betrayal trauma and PTSD, but I emotionally beat myself up for being unable to consistently control my flashbacks and pent-up anger. It's hard to accept the fact that the damage his addiction has caused will not be a quick fix. I'm a go-getter, but I'm running out of patience! I want to be emotionally and physically well *now*.

Since Frank obtained more knowledge about PTSD and betrayal trauma, he understands more about what I'm going through and is exhibiting extreme patience with me. When I hit bottom, he reminds me that this is his fault and sincerely apologizes. Sometimes that helps, but when it doesn't, I go into a tailspin. In my mind, I go through negative events and disturbing images of how he emotionally hurt me with his behavior, and I get upset all over again. This is by far the most difficult part of my recovery.

When I lose control of my emotions, I have to put space between us for a day or so, and he graciously steps away but keeps in touch throughout the day through text messages. He's encouraging and reminds me that I have the strength to fight this. I'm starting to realize that my worst enemy (Frank) has now become my biggest cheerleader.

At this point, I really don't have anything else to put into *Sitting on the Porch Swing* because I'm having a serious struggle with PTSD. I need to focus on my recovery to get it under control. I'm sorry I can't give you the ending of our story yet because I have to stop, put on the armor of God, and fight a war.

PART III: SWEEPING THE PORCH

Chapter 23

SOMEDAY

Someday I will get rid of my anger and hurt
Until then I may get frustrated, cry, and feel sad
I may feel sorry for myself and the pain I'm going through
My heart may still have cracks in it created by an addict
I may scold myself about my inability to be whole again
I may continue to love without receiving it in return
I may sabotage my own recovery to keep peace with the addict
I may mourn for my body that's taken a beating due to stress
I may still give away my heart to those who don't deserve it
I may put myself last to tend to the needs
of others who won't appreciate it

BUT

Someday I will rise up and claim the right to love myself
I will keep my heart safe and be selective of who I give it to
I will not be silent and will stand up for myself
I will not live for other people but only for myself and God
I will live everyday as if it's my last and enjoy life
I will use my God-given talents and be creative in
my arts and crafts
I will play my piano for enjoyment instead
of reaching for the master level
I will not carry others or live for them
I will be grateful for all the blessings God has given me
I will stop focusing on my pain and the past

I WILL LOVE MYSELF AND TAKE MY POWER BACK!

PART III

SWEEPING THE PORCH:

*ENFORCING BOUNDARIES
& RECLAIMING MY INDEPENDENCE*

Chapter 24

SHUT THE DOOR

I have a beautiful rock garden by the patio in the backyard. There are bird houses, trellises, fountains, figurines, flowers, and bird feeders. I put food out for the birds and squirrels and enjoy the scenery while drinking my morning coffee.

In order to keep the squirrels away from the bird seed, I have a baffle on the pole, and in order to keep other animals from coming into the yard, I have a privacy fence. These are boundaries I created for a comfortable and safe environment.

When we raise our children, we create boundaries for their safety. We warn them about running into the street, climbing on furniture, touching the stove, and riding their bikes. But when we're dealing with our adult partners, parents, family members, or friends, it's different. We assume since they're adults we have no right to control their behavior towards us. This couldn't be further from the truth.

Boundaries are not limited to children or "things." It may become necessary to establish boundaries with people who are disrespectful and controlling in order to create healthier relationships.

Since addicts are master manipulators and controllers, I had to learn boundaries to get my power back. Frank and I have been married nineteen years, and over time I allowed him to tear me down emotionally because I wanted to have a happy marriage. I thought if I were a team player and didn't rock the boat, he'd love and respect me more and the addiction would go away. But once the addict gets control, all the love in the world won't matter, so I was fighting a losing battle and giving my power away.

Establishing boundaries is not just for addicts. It can be anyone in your life who disrespects you with the intent of gaining power. If you give them that power, you're the one who will pay the consequences with things such as low self-esteem, unworthiness, depression, and possibly stress-induced health problems.

My counselor Juliane said something profound that I really believe. She said, "When you make the decision to change, people don't like it. They want you to stay in your little box and be quiet because then they don't have to look at themselves." You can ignore someone's behavior if it's not directed at *you*, but when it becomes personal and affects you, there must be boundaries established.

Chapter 25

MY POWERFUL BROOM

Don't panic my friends, I'm not excessive about sweeping. In fact, I have a commercial vacuum cleaner and use a broom only when necessary. Trust me, if that commercial vacuum hose reached into the garage, patio, or front porch, I wouldn't even own a broom! I just needed a catchy title for this chapter.

We sweep walking surfaces to get dirt off so it's not tracked into other areas of our home. I can definitely compare that to the mind and how negative events and thoughts prevent us from having a clear path to think about the good things in our life and have peace. The partner of a sex addict can develop a tome of hurtful and disturbing memories if left unattended, and that's exactly what happened to me.

If I would have set boundaries with Frank earlier and stood up to my mother (whose abuse was my breaking point), I wouldn't have ended up with a compromised immune system and PTSD. Sometimes unconditional love is not returned.

With an addict you *must* keep your power because they won't feel a bit guilty about doing what they have to in order to feed their addiction. Keep in mind, their brain is severely affected like the alcoholic, shopaholic, overeater, drug addict, or any other compulsive behavior to combat some type of emotional disorder like pain or insecurity, and they will do almost anything to get that "fix."

Regardless of how his addiction started, he is indeed responsible for the emotional damage he's done to me and fully accepts the blame. I was a pile of emotional ruins, my health was compromised, and since I was sixty-seven years old, I had accepted the hand I was dealt as a life sentence. I figured I'd just roll with the punches and hope he'd feel sorry for me and change.

Had I not discovered the proper way to set boundaries, I would still be hateful, aggressive, and emotional in an attempt to get him to meet my needs, and that did not work. All I did was put him on the defense.

When you're soft-spoken, calm, direct, and hold your own, it makes a huge difference. They may get ugly and raise their voice, but *if you feed into their anger it's over*. I know because I failed miserably the first few times I tried it, and all I wanted to do was relocate his lips to the nearest wall!

But now I have it down pat because I finally realized I have the right to set boundaries around someone who disrespects me or causes pain. It's been a life-changing experience that's refreshing, and I wish I would have known this earlier in my life because it could have saved me a lot of grief. When you set boundaries, compromise may be necessary, but make sure they don't interfere with your need to feel safe.

Remember, you can argue all day long when both people are on the defense and are determined to win the war by yelling and throwing insults, but the one who continues to argue with a person who has a gentle, calm spirit begins to look foolish. It's tough, but you can master it!

So get your powerful broom out and clear the path to your mind where all the hurtful and negative thoughts dwell. Sweep out all the ugly, replace it with positive thinking, and dream about a future of peace and security. People will control you only if you allow it.

Chapter 26

IDENTIFYING LIMITS

In order to set boundaries, we must first identify what our boundaries are. Before I started this chapter, I sat down and made a list of the things that don't fit into my Christian values, things that cause me emotional discomfort, and situations that upset me. I was disappointed to discover how many things I've not set boundaries around because people assume I'm okay with them. I also realized I'm hesitant to set boundaries around certain areas and need to learn how to do so properly.

I suggest you make your own list to see how successful you've been with setting boundaries and the areas you need to take care of. I've learned so much through counseling and research, so now it's time for me to finish that list. The following are some of the things on my list of boundaries. I'll tell you why I need each one, how I handled the ones I've already set, and my plan for the ones I haven't taken care of yet.

Lying: This is the one that sets me off because I hate to be lied to. I need boundaries around liars because if they lie *to me* I assume they'll lie *about me* and can't be trusted. My first approach is usually something like, "Really? I don't think that's true. Are you sure you have your information straight?" But if I know they're deliberately lying to me, I will say, "That's not true and you know it. Why are you lying to me? If you keep doing this, I'm not going to be able to trust you."

Gossip: Let's be truthful—we've all done it, and this is an area I'm seriously having to work on because of my mother and her abuse toward my sister and me. Mom has become a habitual liar and is still attempting to separate us. We have no idea what her motive is, but I find myself telling people outside of the family everything she's done to me and what a terrible person she is. I need to set boundaries with myself and be selective about who I talk to because it's a family matter. I'm pretty good about not gossiping with my friends, but occasionally I find myself falling into the trap. Sometimes people gossip to get allies, and if you participate you could lose a good friend. I think gossip boundaries are one of the hardest ones to set, but I'll keep working on it.

Politics and Religion: I'm proud to say I excel on these two topics. I don't bring up either subject, but I'll discuss politics or religion with someone if I know they have the same beliefs. I think I need boundaries around these topics because there are so many religions out there that I don't agree with, and politics can be messy. Setting boundaries on these things is easy for me. I just tell people, "Sorry, I don't discuss religion or politics," and I smile.

Arguments: I don't mind productive discussions but hate arguments. I generally do well with boundaries in this category. The rules I set involve no cursing, name calling, or yelling. I think boundaries around arguments (I like to call them discussions) are important because when people raise their voices, nobody listens because they become defensive. I will warn a person once if things get out of hand, and if it continues, I will announce that the conversation is over and that maybe we can continue it later when tempers have calmed down. My boundaries didn't always work with Frank because I broke my own rules and got out of control many times. Now that we're separated, disagreements are handled in a mature manner.

Threats: I rock this one! I set boundaries around threats because I know that's a tactic used to control me. The way I handle it is quite simple. I say, "Are you threatening me? If you are, this conversation is over." That usually shuts them up. I haven't been threatened much in my life but will definitely put a stop to it immediately.

Manipulation and control: I've obviously failed miserably in the past when it came to setting boundaries around this. After all, I stayed with a sex addict for nineteen years and gave away my power, and I also allowed my mother to walk all over me. I think boundaries are needed around manipulation and control because it changes who you are and opens a door to unhappiness, loss of self-esteem, and peace. I've been really successful in this area lately and am getting stronger at exercising my rights, but I do occasionally fall down. I stand up for myself and say no when necessary. I've also learned to watch out for gaslighting and will call Frank out on it.

Sexual groping and uninvited advances: Boundaries need to be set around these because it's my body—I won't allow anyone to take advantage of me. Frank tried this early in the marriage, and it took me about one second to put him in his place. I merely said, "Knock it off and don't touch me that way." I also must have given him "the look" because he totally respects me in that area. But be careful that you don't allow someone to cross that line because it could lead to some serious consequences.

Respect: I was the poster child for someone who was disrespected. I might as well have lain on the floor, taken Frank's foot, and put it on my back. I was pitiful! But respect goes back to manipulation and control. Once you give away your power to someone, they have a green light to treat you however they want to. BUT that's all changed now because I took my power back and was less than a lady when I did. He's tried to disrespect me several times, but after I had my say, it was obvious that he wished he hadn't tried it. The truth is, if you give an addict control, they're happy to take it.

In order to set effective boundaries, you need to know what is acceptable and what makes you uncomfortable. If you feel resentment, it's probably because someone is taking advantage of you. Sometimes we feel guilty and push ourselves too far to meet someone else's expectations, then get upset if we don't feel appreciated.

Setting boundaries may be difficult depending on certain events in your life. If you've been the giver but aren't good at receiving, you may have a hard time exercising your right to set boundaries because you won't expect people to honor them. Allowing people to be dependent on you can have a huge effect because you're seen as the "fixer." You may think people will see you as weak if you need boundaries.

Give yourself the right to set boundaries. Don't be afraid or feel guilty about speaking up or saying no. We allow people to take advantage of us because we don't want to hurt anyone's feelings or be afraid of their response. We'll even drain ourselves emotionally or physically to avoid disappointing someone. Boundaries aren't just about healthy relationships. They're about self-respect. But the biggest key is to follow through and be assertive when someone crosses your boundaries.

Chapter 27

THE CHAINS THAT BIND

I'm infamous for allowing people to take advantage of me and I am hesitant to set boundaries because I don't want to hurt their feelings. I don't mind helping those who appreciate it, but there are a few people in my life who expect me to jump and comply when they snap their fingers. I'll actually rearrange my schedule to accommodate them. I'll be the first to admit that I'm a softie and easily manipulated. That's pretty obvious since now I'm in recovery from letting an addict control me for nineteen years. But things are about to change, my friends!

As you've probably discovered by now, I'm not a professional in the field of boundaries (that's my joke for the day), but I am learning as I go along and hope you'll profit from the fruits of my labor. I have to admit this part is taking more time to write than the first two because I got quite an education about sexual addiction from living with an addict and intensive professional counseling. I wish I would have known more about boundaries years ago because I may not have gotten so sick and ended up with PTSD. But that's water under the bridge now.

I've already set boundaries with Frank, and they're working well so far. It was quite an eye-opener to discover that I have the right to say no. But now I have to learn how to deal with other people in my life who take advantage of me. It's not their fault because I allowed it, but now I have to figure out how to gently but firmly let them know things have changed. Setting boundaries with Frank was easy because at the time I didn't care if the marriage worked or not and had nothing to lose.

Boundaries are healthy because they limit the space between you and others, which allows you to establish guidelines in order to create good relationships. But difficult people with a sense of entitlement can be a challenge because they can be rude and overbearing. Exercising our right to set healthy boundaries gives us the personal freedom to be who we're meant to be and let go of those people who are detrimental to our happiness and peace of mind.

I have a lot of work to do because I'm a "doormat." I'm a caretaker who'll go to extremes to please others and will neglect my own wants and needs in the process. If that's not bad enough, I'm also a "pleaser." I try to avoid conflict at any cost and am not good at standing up for myself. I'm also guilty of absorbing other people's emotions like a sponge and then worrying excessively about them. But, the worst thing I do is tolerate emotional abuse and allow people to disrespect me.

I've excelled at setting boundaries around these things with Frank and am proud of myself. But now I have to set boundaries around other people who disrespect me, and that's not going to be easy because some of them are related to me. In their defense, they assume this is who I am, and it's become natural for them to take advantage of me. Here are some examples of the tactics I plan to use:

- If someone asks me to do something and I'm busy, I will not stop what I'm doing but will say, "I won't be able to do that for you right now, but I'll be available later."

- If someone asks me to do something that I'm not comfortable with, I will say, "I'm sorry, that doesn't work for me."

- If someone tries to start an argument with me, I will say, "I'm not willing to argue with you."

- If someone starts yelling and raising their voice at me, I will say, "I'll be happy to talk to you when you calm down."

- If someone wants to borrow something, I will say, "I'm willing to loan it to you so long as you have it back to me by [whatever date I chose]."

- If someone asks me to take sides in an argument, I will say, "No, I'm not going to get involved because that's between the two of you."

- If I know for a fact that someone is lying to me, I will say, "I know you're not telling the truth, and I'm not interested in anything else you have to say on the matter."

You can't set boundaries without consequences and *must* follow through. Never give consequences that you're not willing or able to stick to. Setting boundaries is not about threats but about giving people choices and consequences for their behavior.

I'm going to list some characteristics of healthy and unhealthy boundaries in relationships with partners. You may not see the signs until things get out of hand, so it could possibly save you a lot of time and grief if you know what to watch out for now.

HEALTHY BOUNDARIES

- Being honest about what you want or need

- Focusing on the best qualities of your partner

- Respecting your differences

- Accepting changes or endings in the relationship

- Being your own person

- Being responsible for your own happiness

- Balancing time together and time apart
- Having friendships outside of the relationship
- Having honest communication
- Being committed to your partner

UNHEALTHY BOUNDARIES

- Being uncomfortable about asking for what you want or need
- Focusing on the worst qualities of your partner
- Blaming your partner for their unique qualities
- Expecting the relationship to never change and being unable to let go
- Feeling incomplete without your partner
- Depending on your partner for your happiness
- Expecting too much togetherness
- Having an inability to have friends outside of the relationship
- Being dishonest, playing emotional games, manipulating
- Lacking commitment and being jealous

This stuff is really pumping me up! I'm ready to break the chains that have had me bound and get the respect I deserve. This chapter has definitely taught me that it's okay to be selfish and set boundaries. In all seriousness, I'm a good person with good morals who loves God dearly, and I know He didn't put me here to be taken advantage of. If I don't do what's necessary to let people know what I need and want, then it will be *my* fault if they continue to use me.

PART III: SWEEPING THE PORCH

Chapter 28

THE OTHER FAMILY

When you get into a relationship, chances are there will be another family you'll need to blend in with. If you're married, there will be in-laws, and if you're just dating, you will still have interactions with each other's family. Sometimes it's a quick and easy transition, but other times it can wreak havoc in your relationship. Unfortunately, I married into a snake pit.

Narcissism, arrogance, manipulation, and control runs deep and wide in Frank's small family. When I started dating him, he had a father who was in a nursing home, one sister, one child, one niece, one great nephew, and a controlling and manipulative ex-wife. I come from a large family of seven, was raised in a close, loving atmosphere, and was taught to respect people and be loving, kind, and giving. Not exactly a match made in Heaven!

When you're in the dating phase, relatives in both families will usually put their best foot forward, and you assume that everything's just hunky-dory. But when the relationship gets serious, you may run into some big problems with the other family. I did, which I talked about in *Get Off My Porch*.

I loved Frank's sister the first time I met her because she seemed genuine and loving, but it didn't take long to see that she had a sense of entitlement and a need to control everyone's life but her own. His ex-wife assumed that she was still the queen (even though she had remarried), and his daughter made it *very* clear that she was indeed the princess. They called the shots, and Frank cowered down to avoid the consequences of being disobedient. It was disturbing to watch. I pointed it out to him many times, but it didn't take long for me to realize I had no place in the marriage—I was just the chambermaid.

I attempted to set boundaries with no luck because Frank catered to their every demand and didn't want to upset them.

So, I was on my own. The only person I was able to deal with successfully was his ex-wife. I was forced to physically threaten her if she didn't stop interfering with our marriage and coming into our home when she pleased (I'm not joking when I say I physically threatened her—sometimes the little Christian girl in me leaves). I'm not proud of that, but nothing else had worked. I had to handle it myself because Frank was a coward.

I met Frank's dad the day he died. He was in a nursing home with Alzheimer's, and Frank previously wouldn't allow me to see him. Since we were just dating at the time I didn't push it, but when he got the call that his dad wouldn't make it through the night, I went there for moral support. After he died, Frank didn't have anything good to say about him, so there was no real father-son relationship. His mother had died before I met him.

The only person in his family who I've been able to have a close and loving relationship with is his niece, but she lives so far away that I don't get to physically see her often. Frank's daughter is not an issue anymore because I eventually gave up and "divorced" her.

Jealousy is a terrible thing, and she refused to share daddy's attention with anyone. Because of this she ruined the chance of having a healthy extended family. She has two children, and I'm not allowed to be involved in their life. They have been ordered to not call me "Grandma." But that's okay because I have three beautiful and loving granddaughters with whom I have an awesome relationship.

I'll bet you're thinking *I would have run like my hair was on fire* after reading about his dysfunctional family. I should have left, but I loved him and really believed things would calm down and everyone would eventually adjust. That saying "time heals all" wasn't true in this case. The only thing time did for me was destroy my self-esteem and peace.

In my case, setting boundaries was impossible because *I didn't know how* and was dealing with extremely dysfunctional people without support from Frank. The mess I married into is not typical, so don't be discouraged. It should be a whole lot easier for you if you're dealing with people who aren't toxic.

Even though I wasn't allowed to be a part of his family, that won't stop me from setting boundaries now where necessary. This old chick is tired of being a kicked dog! I've gained a lot of knowledge on the subject now, but I won't make an effort to heal things with his family because I don't need toxic people in my life.

In order to set effective boundaries with your partner's family (or anyone else for that matter), the first and most important step is getting control of your *own* emotions of fear, anger, and love. You may not have thought about it, but you *already* have the ability to control your emotions—you've done it all your life in situations like physical pain, hurt feelings, rejection, and other disappointing events. *The key to controlling emotions is to be logical and think before you act.*

Before you set boundaries with their family, decide what type of boundaries you need and what will or will not work for you. Speak in the first person (for example, "I need," "I feel," "I agree"), which puts you in a good position and gives you strength.

You and your partner need to make the decision on which areas of your life you're willing to share with their family before boundaries are set. They don't need to know every aspect of your relationship such as finances, debt, disagreements, or other personal matters. Some secrets shouldn't be shared because they may be used as ammunition against you later.

Be careful about attacking or insulting their family and focus on what your needs are. You may even want to point out the good things you see in their family instead of the negative to show your sincerity about having a better relationship.

Always be ready to follow through and be firm about the boundaries you've set. Hold your ground to show you're serious. If you don't, they may feel they have the ability to pressure you into changing your mind and giving in. At that point, you've given them control.

If boundaries are not respected and they don't comply with your requests, you better have a plan to turn things back around. This can be done easily if you're polite yet firm, and eventually they may get the point and give up. Remember, there are some people who will not back down, so if the situation gets out of control, you can turn around and walk away. That makes the statement that you're not going to argue and have made up your mind.

Since this is your partner's family and they know their family better than you do, let them take the lead and decide which approach would be more effective. If your partner isn't on board with the boundaries you need, it will not work and their family will assume *you're* the one with the problem.

If you've been unsuccessful with setting boundaries with their family and the relationship is spiraling out of control, you may have to walk away like I did because it can take a toll on your emotions and physical well-being.

PART III: SWEEPING THE PORCH

Chapter 29

TOXIC FAMILY MEMBERS

Family ties are the most important relationships you'll ever have. If you're one of the lucky ones, your immediate family will stay close and committed forever. But unfortunately that's not always the case. Sometimes it only takes *one person* to destroy these precious bonds. It breaks my heart when I say that person was my mother.

Growing up and as adults, our family was inseparable. We were like a pack of wolves. If you messed with one, you'd have to deal with all of us. We trusted each other completely, and there was never a question of feeling loved and accepted by each and every member. If someone had a need, we came together as a family and took care of it.

When my dad died, we all rallied around my mom and took care of her needs. My parents lived in a senior complex at the time, and plans were made to relocate my mom because she was depressed. My aunt was a realtor and found a house two blocks away from Frank and me, so she was able to have family nearby. At the time, one of my brothers was disabled from a plane crash and lived in Alabama, my other brother lived in California, and my two sisters lived in rural areas.

Frank and I were happy that she lived so close. We kept in contact daily, tended to her yard and anything she needed, and were there for emotional support. My sisters visited her when they were in town and were always willing to help out, so everything flowed easily. My brother who lives in California visits twice a year, and he spent a lot of time with Mom when he was home. So, she didn't lack attention from her children. But somewhere along the way things took an ugly turn.

To this day, I still don't know what I did to deserve the emotional traumatic pain she has inflicted on me. Maybe she was unhappy and needed someone to take it out on, and I was the closest one to her. In my research, I've read that a toxic person will harm the one they're the closest to because they know you will have a hard time removing yourself—especially if you're family. And if it's a parent, it's even worse.

Her emotional abuse started over ten years ago over something so insignificant it was unbelievable. I didn't go to a graduation party for my niece, and she vehemently lied to my sister about the reason I didn't attend. The truth is, we had been in Colorado and came home to a flooded finished basement and had a disaster on our hands. Mom was keeping an eye on our house and didn't let us know until our plane home landed, so the water sat in there for days, which created more destruction and, eventually, mold.

If that wasn't bad enough, she lied to my other two siblings, as well as some relatives whom I was close to, so everyone turned against me. That was by far the most emotional pain I've ever experienced in my life. I was so depressed after a few months that I sent a letter to everyone in the family and disconnected.

In that letter, I pointed out all the flaws *they* had in an attempt to defend myself for a "crime" I hadn't committed. I regret sending it now, but most of the negative things I said about my siblings came from the lies Mom had told me about *them*. I was so devastated and desperate that I didn't know what else to do. We all eventually came back together, but we'll never recover the time we lost as a family.

What kind of parent intentionally sets out to separate their children? Perhaps she was jealous of our relationships and felt the need to destroy them so she would get more attention. Mom didn't have a reputation of being a liar and neither did I, but everyone fell in line and believed her since she was "Mom." But that's not the end of the story.

Mom and I eventually came back together. Things seemed to be going well, but she attacked me again last fall with more lies. At that point, I had to permanently end the relationship. This emotional rollercoaster she's had me on has caused so much grief, confusion, and pain that I can't let her manipulation and control destroy my happiness and affect my health anymore.

Her first attack ten years ago caused severe health problems for me because I couldn't get an emotional handle on the situation. Yes, Frank and I were having some serious problems that caused a lot of stress, but I could have gotten through that with a divorce. To have your own mother turn against you was too much.

She's made it clear that she won't own the lies and continues to play the victim. She's starting to get a bad reputation because people are beginning to see through her now, but I can't help her anymore. She'd rather lose a daughter than confess to the lies she's told. I can't imagine doing that to one of my children. I absolutely have to stay away from her now because I can't put my health in jeopardy again. But the one thing I do is pray for her and put her in God's hands.

Being a parent *does not* give you a pass to abuse your children without consequences. You may be in charge when they're younger, but as adults you lose the power to control them. I have walked away with a clear conscience and have absolutely no guilt because I treated her with dignity and respect. I don't hate my mother and will cherish the good years, but she *chose* to repeatedly mistreat me and will continue to do so if I allow it.

It's difficult to deal with toxic family members. They create drama and drain you because of conflicting feelings, betrayal, and anger. They'll take advantage of the bond that's supposed to be loving and respectful and will manipulate you. They assume you won't leave under *any* circumstances because you're family. I truly believe that a toxic parent can do the most damage in a family because as children we're taught to trust and respect them. You continuously try to understand and forgive their behavior because it's your family. Unspoken bonds in families make their abuse more painful because you feel you must keep a positive relationship with the abuser, regardless of how they treat you.

Taking that step to let go is incredibly difficult but necessary if the abuser refuses to step up and do what's right. Like I've said before, I didn't choose to be her daughter, but I can walk away from her abuse. I hope and pray that Mom doesn't succeed in turning any of my siblings against me again, but if she does, there's nothing I can do about it. The biggest comfort I have is that God knows the truth, and that's enough for me.

Toxic family members will verbally and sometimes physically attack you when you're alone with them or on a telephone conversation, so it becomes your word against theirs. In addition, they will most likely play the victim and cry wolf in case you tell someone. They will hide their behavior and manipulate your feelings because of the intimate relationship a family has. If it's a parent, people tend to believe them because you're just the child. You must remember that *they're the one with the problem*, but sometimes that doesn't make it any better.

If you have any notion of fixing this person, you're wasting your time because there's something amiss inside of them that they take it out on others. They may not know themselves why they behave that way, but it doesn't justify their cruel behavior. Toxic people are aware of the disruption they cause and are usually negative individuals, but that doesn't mean you have to tolerate their behavior. Once they start on you, the chances of them stopping are slim to none because they gain a sense of power over you.

There comes a time when you have to assess the situation and decide if it's interfering with your peace of mind and happiness. You may have to keep your distance and spend less time with them or disconnect completely. It's painful when you discover that a family member isn't capable or doesn't love you the way you love them. Obviously, their relationship with you isn't built on unconditional love or respect.

If you get to the point where you've had enough, keep in mind that you have a right to be happy. I *allowed* my mother to disrespect me and was afraid to stand up to her for a long time. When I finally did, she got more aggressive and dead set on punishing me. She started gathering allies by accusing me of hurting *her* in order to isolate me so that these people would treat me badly, and unfortunately, some of them did. She painted me as the perpetrator and herself as the victim.

Toxic people have no problem lying or making up stories to turn the truth around. This redirection is manipulation to punish whoever confronted them and destroy their reputation in the process. But sometimes it backfires because they get confused about the lies they've told, and people start seeing them for who they really are. But at that point, the damage is done and they've lost a family member because the trust is gone.

It's okay to walk away from a family member—even a parent. Your forgiveness will not fix the person who's hurting you because they get some type of satisfaction from being able to control you, even if they have to instill some type of pain to get that control. You may also lose other family members in the process because they've chosen to believe the lies, especially if they come from a parent. And sometimes there are people who are not willing to listen to your side. I know because when I tried to defend myself, most of the people believed me, but there were a few who didn't want to hear that my mom was the guilty one.

To this day, I feel a distance when I'm around the people who believe Mom, and it makes me sad because I was so close to them. Mom still continues to feed the fire by creating more lies to keep her allies in line and avoid any chance that they may reestablish a relationship with me. I only hope that someday they'll learn the truth. But what they don't realize is they may be the next target because toxic people *must always* have control of *someone* to feel superior.

Since I've permanently severed the relationship with my mother, my stress level has come down substantially because there won't be any conversations she can turn around to use against me. It was hard to walk away, but she forced me to by treating me like I didn't belong to her. If I thought for one minute that I'd done something to one of my sons to make them walk away, I'd be devastated and would move heaven and earth to make it right. My mother is not physically gone, but I don't know this person who resides in her body now. Setting a boundary was necessary.

PART III: SWEEPING THE PORCH

Chapter 30

FEAR OF SETTING BOUNDARIES

If you're like I was, the thought of setting boundaries on someone is pretty frightening. My first thought was that I'd lose someone I loved or a special friend. I would be on that "list" of inconsiderate troublemakers, the word would get out, and I would get a bad reputation.

I believe the people who know me well would describe me as an easygoing gal who doesn't like any type of dissension and will do anything to avoid an argument. I choose friends who have a good sense of humor, love unconditionally, and believe in God. I'm proud to say that I have eight good friends, and I love them dearly. Some of them have been my friends for over thirty years. We can express our feelings and talk openly about our problems without fear of being judged. We're there for each other unconditionally and trust each other completely.

Before the separation, I tried to set boundaries on Frank, but I gave up after he ignored them. However, once I discovered I had a *right* to set boundaries and learned how to do it properly, things changed. It's made a huge difference in our relationship.

At that time, I was still afraid of setting boundaries on my mother because she had absolutely no remorse about what she'd done and seemed to enjoy punishing me. I knew she was capable of lying and was looking for any opportunity to destroy my reputation. I finally realized that the people who believed her didn't matter because those who love me and know me well would question her accusations and not get involved.

Mom lives a few blocks away from me, and occasionally we run into each other. Since I made the decision to permanently separate from her last December, there have been incidents

ENFORCING BOUNDARIES & RECLAIMING MY INDEPENDENCE

where she was in the same store, snuck up behind me, and attempted to start an argument. In the past, I quickly walked away because I was so intimidated and hurt by her hateful looks and cruel words. I was afraid to set boundaries and still allowed her to control my emotions, even though we are estranged.

A few days ago, she once again approached me in a store, spoke harshly, and glared at me like I was her worst enemy. The look on her face was absolute hatred. She actually looked demented, and it sent a chill up my spine. I honestly believe she would have physically attacked me if given the opportunity at that moment. Any chance of reconciliation is gone now. I never want to see her again and will definitely not put myself in a situation where I'm alone with her. If she ever approaches me in public again, I intend to video the encounter on my phone and ask for an order of protection.

Even though her goal was to intimidate me, I verbally stood up to her, and it felt good to take my power back. I finally got the perfect opportunity to set boundaries and did so with just three words before walking away. I wasn't hateful—I was direct. She will *never* manipulate and control me again. She made the decision to throw me away with her continuous emotional abuse. But what she doesn't realize is there are a lot of family and friends who are more than happy to catch me.

I'll never understand what deranged thoughts went through her head when she made the decision to intentionally separate my sister and me. We're together again, which is great, but since I disconnected from Mom, I feel like my other sister and brother are pulling away from me. That really hurts. I know they talk to Mom and probably feel sorry for her, but this time I'll make no attempt to defend myself. I don't expect them to understand my emotions or the choices I've had to make to have peace because it didn't happen to them. Maybe someday all us siblings can come together and be the happy family we used to be.

I've been studying different types of dementia and psychological disorders to try and find out if there's something mentally wrong with her, but she doesn't fit into any of the categories because she's able to manipulate, premeditate, and remember lies she's told. She was tested last year for her memory and passed with flying colors. The only conclusion I can come up with is that she's an unhappy woman and is punishing me in order to make herself feel better. I don't want her to have a mental problem, but if she did, it would explain a lot.

"Love thy mother" had always been easy until she started mistreating me, but I know God doesn't expect me to take her abuse but to stand up for myself. Even Jesus got mad in the temple! I walked out of that store with a peace that passes understanding. I talked to God for a few minutes, turned on my Christian music, and sang. Setting boundaries that day set me free from the Hell my mother had put me in.

I discovered in my research that bullies take advantage of your kindness and generosity because you allow them to. These people have a way of turning your "no" into a "yes" by talking behind your back and accusing you of being spoiled, selfish, and unreasonable. Rather than hold your ground, you give in because you don't want to be "labeled." Well, I will stick a label on them right now—they're takers who aren't interested in giving.

These controllers and manipulators know a soft target when they see it and will continue to use you unless you set boundaries. Compromise is not usually possible with bullies and will more than likely provoke them because they're not getting what they want. Bullies are usually angry individuals, so you need to remember that *they're* the ones who have a problem. You don't have to give in to their demands.

Maintaining boundaries with other people teaches them to respect you. Don't allow their anger to force you to give in to their demands. If they get mad, don't feed the fire and argue—just do nothing. It seems that silence is golden in these situations because it takes two people to fight, so take the high road.

Fear of setting boundaries is normal. You may be afraid of rejection, judgment, embarrassment, or a possible confrontation with the individual. Remind yourself that there is a reason why you need to set boundaries with this person—you have a right to protect yourself and not be disrespected. You need to be assertive without being rude—be calm and firm and say as few words as possible. Don't justify your decision or apologize for the boundary you need to set because that will send a mixed message and suggest you're not serious.

Their reaction to your request for boundaries could be civil, or they may become argumentative and aggressive. If they do, just remember that *your* behavior in that moment must reflect the boundaries you're setting. Don't feel guilty and let anxiety prevent you from following through. Enforcing boundaries will build up your confidence and self-esteem and let others know that you're serious and don't intend to back down.

Unfortunately, boundaries will not work with everyone, and you may have to walk away if they continue to cause unnecessary stress and anxiety. But would it really be so bad if you didn't have to put up with their behavior? I don't know about you, but I don't need or want that type of relationship. The peace of not having to deal with the trauma can be wonderful, so nothing's really been lost.

I'm not going to try to change someone who doesn't want to change or give repeated chances to a controller or manipulator. I'm going to watch how they act instead of listening to what they say. I won't be in a relationship anymore with someone who takes and gives nothing. I'm not going to cause myself pain anymore by staying in a toxic relationship. I'm going to be happy and have peace, and if some people get lost in the shuffle, so be it. As long as I stay close to God, my world will be just fine.

After all, **fear** is just "**f**alse **e**vidence **a**ppearing **r**eal."

Chapter 31

THE "S" WORD

We live in a fast-paced world where we've been taught to believe that there are not enough hours in a day to get everything done. People wake up with a list in their head of the tasks they must perform and usually feel overwhelmed before they even get out of bed. Their feet hit the floor and off they go!

After I retired, I was afraid I'd get bored, so I filled my days with projects around the house, started doing a lot of crafts, became a licensed jewelry designer, and started a business. I did weekend markets, sold from a website, had displays in local shops, and donated jewelry to many charities. It was an extremely profitable business, but suddenly it became a real job. There were times when I had to make a hundred pieces in a week to keep up with the demands. I worked my business for ten years before I realized it was time to quit because it wasn't fun anymore and was causing a lot of bad stress.

There are two types of stress—good and bad. The good stress comes in handy when we need to react quickly to a threatening or emergency situation. The bad stress is created by the pressures of everyday life and social situations, such as arguments in the family, finances, jobs, traffic, disrespectful people, health problems, and a myriad of other negative things. But once the stress becomes chronic, it can create a mountain of health problems if left unattended.

In a stressful situation, our body releases the hormones cortisol and adrenaline, which cause our lungs to pump oxygen quickly into the bloodstream and raise our heartbeat and blood pressure in order to avoid the stressor. If you don't learn how to control stress, eventually your body won't be able to function properly, and you may end up with high blood pressure and possibly some serious health problems. I speak from experience because my stress got so bad that I ended up with a compromised immune system, which can be very dangerous.

Obesity has become an epidemic, and people with chronic stress are getting so desperate that they'll do anything to lose weight but have no success. What they don't realize is that the stress hormone cortisol *increases* your appetite because the body needs energy. Stress hormones also make it difficult for your pancreas to secrete insulin, which gets glucose out of your blood and into your cells. So as you can see, eating more sugar to get energy is counterproductive and will cause you to gain weight.

It's true that burning fat causes weight loss. However, fat burning becomes difficult if you have chronic stress because your cells need oxygen to metabolize fat into energy. But the bad news is stress keeps oxygen from getting to the cells, so carbohydrates are used to produce energy and sugar cravings take over.

I put together some of the health issues you may run into if you don't get control of your stress. This is a short list, but believe me, there's a lot of damage stress can cause—even death! Maybe it will make you think about the consequences you'll have to deal with if you don't get serious about kicking this disorder to the curb. Here is the list:

- Immune disorders
- Fatigue
- Appetite changes
- Headaches/Migraines
- Digestive issues
- Chronic fatigue syndrome

- Muscle pain
- Insomnia
- Heart Attack/Stroke/Chest pains
- Depression
- Low sex drive
- Upset stomach
- High blood pressure
- Irritable bowel syndrome
- Hypothyroidism
- Joint inflammation
- Difficulty concentrating
- Weight gain

Do I have your attention *now*?

I personally don't believe in taking antidepressants unless it's *absolutely necessary,* and it should be short term while you work through the problems that caused your stress or depression. I had chronic stress and was so messed up that I didn't even know where to start until I took it upon myself to do some serious research on the subject. I'm going to tell you some of the things I've done that have worked for me, and perhaps they will help you too. I suggest that you come up with a plan of your own that will bring your stress level down because if your health starts failing, you're going to wish you had.

Trust me, I know because when I look back, I allowed people to mistreat me because I didn't have the guts to set boundaries and stand up for myself. I got upset over small things that really didn't matter. I *expected* to have a bad day and stopped looking at the good things in my life. I had a private "poor little ole me" pity party *every day*, which kicked my stress level up even higher.

But the worst thing I did was give up on me. When I finally got desperate and asked God to show me how to *help myself* instead of whining to him about how mistreated and unhappy I was, everything changed. I was on a mission to save myself, and I'm proud to say I did. *I am a child of God and was not put here to be abused.* Of course, some people are still in shock because something's seriously wrong with Cat—she's just not herself. I take that as a compliment, thank you very much!

Don't get me wrong, I still get stressed sometimes because of our situation, but I'm serious about self-care now. I've gone through a lot of trauma, but I will win this fight. It's getting easier every day. I refuse to put my health in jeopardy again, so it's my turn to be selfish!

Lack of sleep will cause stress, especially if you're up half the night worrying or having negative thoughts. I relied on sleeping pills for over eighteen years. Yes, I slept, but during the day I was so groggy that I couldn't function. And to top it off, I drank soda like water to get more energy, which was a bad choice! Now I will occasionally take melatonin if my mind gets too messy, which is a more natural option, but I don't rely on it. I avoid too much caffeine, and if I want a soda, it's usually 7UP, orange juice, or a Gatorade (although occasionally I treat myself to an extremely unhealthy, caffeine-loaded, sugar-filled Coke or Pepsi. What can I say, I still love 'em!).

I start relaxing two or three hours before I go to bed. I watch some of the evening news, but if it gets depressing, I switch channels and watch comedies or other uplifting shows. I'm a baseball junkie, so if there's a game on I'm so tuned in there's no room for bad thoughts. The little girl in me still likes to color, so I have a variety of the adult coloring books (calm down, it's not the type of "adult" you think) that have circular mandalas, nature scenes, and other designs that help me relax and bring out my artistic side. These books are popular and were created to relieve stress and calm your mind—they really work for me.

After my mind is relaxed, I recline and snuggle up with my dog Miss Babette, focus on her innocent face for a few minutes, and remember what unconditional love is. If a bad thought from the past pops up, I tell myself that *it is only a memory and not a present danger*. The past will haunt you forever if you allow it to. I don't always get a handle on it, but it's getting easier because I'm able to push the ugly thoughts out more quickly.

I made the commitment to physically get in bed at a certain time every night whether I am sleepy or not and set my alarm to get up at the same time each morning. There are some long nights where I am up and down wrestling with past events, but over time, my body has acclimated and I have a good schedule. And most importantly, I have changed my nightly prayer. I start my prayers by telling God everything I'm grateful for, which keeps me focused on the good things in life. Then I pray for my loved ones, and I end my prayer with "thy will be done."

People forget to be grateful. Instead, they focus on their problems and forget about the many, many blessings they have received. As I sit here right now, I see the beautiful home I live in. I know there's a bright red Dodge Charger sitting in the garage (yep, granny's a sports car girl). My dog Miss Babette is snoozing on the couch, and even though she's fourteen years old, she's healthy.

I have two sons, one daughter-in-law, a new daughter-in-law coming into the family next year, and three beautiful granddaughters who are healthy and love me very much. I have a husband who loves me even though he's struggling with an addiction right now. I have food in the fridge, four phones in the house, two televisions, beautiful furniture and fixtures, money to buy natural supplements to keep myself healthy, and if I keep going, this book is going to be very thick! But one of the most important things I have now is my health.

I'd like for you to stop reading right now and make two lists. For the first one, list the things you're grateful for right down to your toothbrush, and take your time. For the second list, record the negative things in your life. If you're honest, the first list should be much longer than the second. I rest my case. I just remembered about a book my older brother gave me years ago named *Don't Sweat the Small Stuff... It's All Small Stuff*. I loved that book, and it got me through some rough times. But evidently it ended up on the bookshelf. I need to find that little book and read it again.

Something else that's helped me a lot is cardiovascular exercise (walking, taking the stairs, riding a bike, etc.), which metabolizes stress hormones to keep my body and mind calm. Plus, I'm losing weight. Don't go crazy with it though—you don't have to run on the treadmill for two hours. But if you can accumulate a total of one hour throughout the day, you'll be amazed at the benefits. Trust me, I was a certified personal trainer, and I'm educated on the subject. The trick is to *keep your body moving* because the term "move it or lose it" is true. I have to admit that I got away from it because of depression, but now I'm back at it and am reaping the benefits.

Try to carve out a few minutes each day to just relax. Close your eyes and think of the positive things in your life. If bad thoughts intrude, kick them out by saying things like "I'm calm and relaxed, and there's no room for negative thoughts right now." As you're relaxing, inhale and exhale slowly and try to let your body go limp. This is an excellent technique. If you know how to meditate, by all means do so.

Talking to someone you trust can help tremendously because it distracts you from stress and releases tension. Some people choose to keep a diary for a short time to figure out what triggers their stress so they can avoid certain situations and learn better coping skills. And the last thing I suggest is to learn time management and get your priorities straight. Sometimes we feel overwhelmed, and that's a common cause of stress. Admit that you can't do everything and need time for yourself to just relax.

I had to set boundaries on *myself* in order to have some downtime to relax. I have a calendar book that takes two pages to display one week, and each day has a large area to write on. I circle my priorities for that day in green, and the not-so-important things are carried over to the next day if I *choose* not to do them. This was difficult for me to master because I thought everything was a priority and that I was a failure if I didn't complete the list every day.

But I learned to say the beautiful word "no." I no longer run at a breakneck speed to please everyone else, especially the ones who don't appreciate it. The biggest lesson I learned is people will take advantage of you as long as you allow it. I'm not a robot, and I'm not here to serve anyone but God. I will always be available in an emergency if possible, but I've made a commitment to set boundaries when necessary. I did this to myself, and now it's time to slow down and enjoy my life. Unhealthy stress is now my nemesis, and I will defeat it!

PART III: SWEEPING THE PORCH

Chapter 32

DON'T DRINK THE POISON!

Have you ever been around people who can ruin your day by just showing up? You can be in the best of moods, but you feel exhausted and worn out after spending time with them. These people will make you feel bad about yourself by saying or doing something critical. They will cut you down, give hateful looks, be sarcastic, or accuse you of doing something you didn't do. If you dare stand up to them, they will immediately blame you and make it your fault. By the time you leave, you feel emotionally drained and sometimes physically ill.

These people are toxic and can actually be dangerous to the point of threatening your peace of mind and health. In other words, they're *poisonous* because their behavior can lead to stress, depression, and anxiety. They're annoying, obnoxious, and depressing to be around. They can ruin your reputation and self-esteem, get you fired from your job, destroy relationships with your family and friends, and make your life unbearable.

It's not hard to spot these individuals if you know what to look for. Sometimes you don't realize they're toxic, but over time, it will become evident because their true selves will eventually be revealed.

The following is a list of some common types of toxic individuals and their characteristics:

Manipulator: These people are all about control and will actually make a plan ahead of time to get what they want. They are cunning and capable of lying, accusing, and playing the victim. They have no guilt about emotionally hurting anyone.

Slanderer: This is one of the most toxic individuals because their lies can destroy your reputation and life. But they're easy to spot because they talk about other people behind their backs, so you can be assured they will most definitely be talking about you.

Pathological Liar: I have a real knack for spotting these poisonous creatures because I personally know a few pathological liars. They can look me straight in the eyes and lie to my face without even blinking. If I confront them about the lie—even if I have proof—they will tell yet another lie to cover up the first one. The look on their face after they've lied says, "Take that!" These people have lied *to me* and *about me*. Unfortunately, I do have to see them on occasion, so the only way I can deal with it is to stay away from them as much as possible and be selective about the topics I discuss. I guess they think there are only nine Commandments, right?

Naysayer: If you want to have a bad day, hang out with one of these. Insecurity, which can be caused by jealousy or hatred, runs deep with these unpleasant individuals. They find fault with everyone and everything and see no joy in life. If you're around them too long, they can quickly bring you down and ruin your good mood.

Drama Queen/King: These emotional train wrecks are always ticked off about something, are dramatic, and don't have the ability to calm down long enough to handle their life. If there's a crisis, they blow things way out of proportion, and if there's not a crisis, they will create one. They talk endlessly about their trauma and drama but have no interest in anyone else's life.

Psychopath: There are two personalities in a psychopath—the good and the evil. They can be charming and alluring, but underneath it they have no compassion, empathy, sympathy, or conscience. They enjoy watching people suffer with no remorse whatsoever. Most psychopaths are abusive and can cause a lot of damage, even death if provoked. Since they're so charismatic, it may take a while before you see what lies beneath the charm, but when you do, stay away from them!

Blackmailer: Run hard and run fast because these people are extremely dangerous. They work to gain your trust so you will divulge your secrets and weaknesses. They're jealous individuals and will pretend to be your friend while developing a plan to take you down. If you cross them, they will threaten to expose the information they've gathered about you if you don't give them what they want.

Bully: Being the center of attention is usually the goal of a bully. They get a rush out of intimidating someone in front of a crowd to feed their ego. Their hateful look can be scary because you don't know if they will actually carry out their threats.

Agitator: The agitator enjoys arguments. They're the ones who purposely give an opposing view or ask hateful questions to get a person upset to the point where they feel the need to defend themselves, which can create an argument. Once the fight starts, the agitator enjoys the chaos and then will accuse you of being too sensitive.

Sponge: These people are usually looking for money or anything else you may have that they want. They seem to lose their memory when it's time to pay back and are conveniently not able to return favors.

Kill-joy: This annoying individual will almost always be in a bad mood and whine to anyone who'll listen. They'll tell you about every negative thing that's happened to them and have a way of predicting the negative events of the future. They will hold on to their bad mood because they get attention, but if you try to cheer them up, it won't matter because they'll have a negative response to that too.

After doing research for this chapter, I got a little stressed just *reading* about the different types of toxic people. As I typed this chapter, I realized that I know quite a few people who fit into some of these categories, so I've learned right along with you. It seems that I need to be more watchful around a few people and see if their behavior does, in fact, affect me.

When I say, "Don't drink the poison," I mean don't put yourself in a position to allow toxic individuals to affect your peace of mind—no matter who it is!

Chapter 33

TAKE CONTROL OF YOUR SANITY

Learning how to separate the addict from the man was difficult for me, but now I realize it's the most valuable and powerful tool I have. I still struggle with it sometimes because I see Frank as the carrier of evil behavior. He appears to be getting stronger in his fight against the addict, but I know he's not cured yet.

I may have just brought up a few eyebrows when I used the word "cured" because it seems to be a common belief that an addiction is a lifetime sentence. I'm going to be bold right now and say I don't believe that. I will also stand on my belief that God can heal us if we truly turn our problems over to him and have faith. I'm living proof of the statements I just made, and no one will ever make me believe that God hasn't been there for me.

As you know, I've had some serious health issues in the past caused by emotional abuse from the addict and my mother that could have totally disabled me, but I'm healthier now than I was five years ago. I have to admit there were times when I fell on my face and gave up, but something inside kept telling me to stand back up and fight. *I know beyond a shadow of a doubt* it was God pushing me forward because there was a time when I thought death would have been better than what I was going through. I was so emotionally beat up that I just didn't care anymore, but everything changed when I *seriously* reached out to him.

I've come a long way and learned so much, but I still struggle with intrusive images and negative thinking from the past. My counselor mentioned "cognitive behavior therapy" (hereafter referred to as CBT) as a way to help me control my thoughts and behaviors when triggers pop up with my PTSD. Cat's digging in and researching again, so let's learn together, shall we?

CBT can be extremely beneficial because it may help you deal with adverse situations quickly by changing how you feel, think, and react. It can help with various emotional problems including anxiety and depression. The reason I've chosen to research this is because it's effective for PTSD. I'm one of those unfortunate people who are emotionally vulnerable, so I'm really excited about using this technique. Healthy thinking can have a positive effect on how you respond and behave. If you're committed to the process, it can become a positive lifestyle change.

Some of the things I'm excited about learning are how to handle bad memories from the past, intrusive images, and my self-esteem. 2 Corinthians 10:5 talks about "taking every thought captive," and that's my goal. It amazes me every time I find a scripture that assures me I'm on the right track. I love the old anagram of the word *Bible*, which is "**B**asic **I**nstructions **B**efore **L**eaving **E**arth." *We are all in charge of our own sanity and shouldn't let other people's behavior affect our well-being and peace of mind!*

Frank just called me about a sermon he was watching, and the scripture that jumped out at him was Psalm 27:10 "Though my father and mother forsake me, the Lord will receive me." My dad never mistreated me, but my mom's emotional abuse after my dad passed on still haunts me every day. I can't believe this is the same person who helped raise me and was so loving and caring. But I know God loves me unconditionally, and that will never change.

My younger sister is having a hard time emotionally because Mom's attacking her now, so I spent time trying to comfort her yesterday. Since I've been dealing with Mom's betrayal on and off for ten years, I was able to convince her that she was the victim and did nothing wrong—just like I was. We both agreed that we need one question answered: why has Mom treated us this way? She has four living children but treats our other siblings well. We may never know, but we intend to move forward and keep the morals and values that we learned growing up because that's what made us such a close family. Dad's gone now, but we know he would be proud of us. We want to honor him, and it's the right thing to do.

As I held her while she cried, I can honestly say I felt her pain of Mom's betrayal. She's been a good daughter just like I was and doesn't deserve this. I warned her about stress and how it could affect her health. Since mom's abuse toward her was recent, she's still trying to handle the reality of it all. I'm glad it happened to me first, so I can be there for her now. As I learn about CBT techniques, I will teach her so she won't have to go through as much pain as I have. I pray for her daily and will be there when she needs me because that's what families are supposed to do.

Our emotions are often controlled by our thinking. Sometimes in a bad situation our mind will immediately go to the worst case scenario even though we don't know all the details—we just assume it's going to turn out bad. At that point we can become stressed out. I am certainly guilty of this type of behavior, but I need to defend myself because I was living with an addict and have a mother who apparently doesn't love me anymore.

Over time, I realized the outcome would always be bad with these two people because they knew I was easily manipulated and quick to forgive. These cowards took out their frustrations on me in order to make themselves feel better to feed their ego because *they're* insecure. I expected a bad outcome, and they never let me down. Unfortunately, this negative thinking still affects me even though Frank has moved out and I've *chosen* to end the relationship with my mom. Almost every day I dwell on the lies that are being told about me and Frank by my mother and a few relatives, and I can't control my thoughts. This is why I'm so excited about CBT. I *will* conquer this!

CBT uses the "thinking-feeling-acting" paradigm. It focuses on helping people think more realistically instead of heading straight to the negative self-defeating thoughts. I really love what Woodrow Wilson said: "He who does not control his thoughts does not control his life." Truer words were never spoken! Keep in mind that negative thinking can lead to depression, which is never a good place to be. Your thinking will trigger a feeling, and you will most likely act on that feeling.

Here are a few examples of what I call "stinking thinking" to give you an idea how it's easy to set yourself up for failure:

Overgeneralizing is when something negative happens to you once and you assume it will continue to happen again and again. For example, if a waiter is extremely rude to you, then you may come to the conclusion that *all* waiters will be that way. But if you stop and think about it, you'll realize that you've had a lot of waiters who were very kind. You have to put the situation into perspective and see "specific" situations rather than "general" situations.

Over exaggeration is when we take *one event* and totally blow it out of proportion. With little evidence, we assume the outcome is going to be terrible. For example, you meet someone, set up a date, and they're late. You may automatically assume you've been played for a fool because they really aren't attracted to you and changed their mind. Or, you may think they've been in an accident. At that point you need to ask yourself if you have any evidence to support your thoughts. Usually the answer is no. Gear your thoughts down a bit—they could have just been dealing with heavy traffic.

Mind reading is a popular flaw in negative thinking. People assume they know what someone else is thinking, even though the other person hasn't shared their thoughts. Mind readers assume that others think negatively about them and have negative intentions. These thoughts could actually be coming from your own insecurity. If you need to validate your thoughts, ask questions—don't just assume.

Predicting the future is an ugly one for me because I'm guilty of this cognitive distortion. However, I only seem to kick into this stinking thinking with Frank and my mother because they've both mistreated me, and I expect they always will.

I almost always kick into this gear with Mom when I hear the horrific lies she's still telling about me, and I have now accepted the fact that she's determined to destroy my reputation. I now realize that I can't do anything to stop her wagging tongue, so I have to control my own emotions. Unfortunately, the only way I can handle my emotions about her is to believe she's gone—not dead, but not the mother I loved so much.

The few relatives she has in her "corner" are not an issue anymore because I realize they're as tainted as she is, so I just stay away from them as much as possible. One of the most valuable lessons I've learned from writing my books is that I can choose who I want to be in my life, and I can step away from the cruel ones because they're toxic.

Frank is a different issue though. Since we're attempting to renew our friendship, we're spending a lot of time together. He tells me that he's doing well and not objectifying women anymore, but when we go out in public, my old behavior kicks in. I rarely look at his face because I expect I'll see him staring at women, so I'm not giving him the chance to prove himself. I'm definitely predicting the future outcome every time, so I stay on guard. CBT teaches you how to take risks and remind yourself that past experiences don't necessarily dictate the future.

I only gave you a few examples of cognitive distortions, but I truly believe cognitive behavior therapy is going to be a turning point for me once I learn it. If you own it and rethink it, you can release it. I strongly encourage you to check it out!

PART III: SWEEPING THE PORCH

Chapter 34

SUMMARY

Well, this book was certainly a learning experience for me, and I hope you gathered some valuable information too. I have to admit that I'm a little apprehensive about setting some boundaries around a few people who I didn't realize *may* be affecting my mood when I'm around them. As the opportunity presents itself, I'm going to start paying attention to them and really focus on how or *if* their behavior is detrimental to me. If I find that I don't get anxious around them and can handle things with no emotional issues, I'll let it go but will still test the waters from time to time.

I know I'm supposed to "fear not," but I'm a human being and this boundary thing is new to me. I'm sure God understands. Actually, I'm starting to feel more confident about setting boundaries. I've been through a whole lot, and I have to stand up for myself and stop allowing people to mistreat me and take advantage of my good nature and kindness. If they walk away from me, I haven't lost anything because then I'll know they were selfish and just using me.

I'm not going to just walk up to them and say something like "I'm setting boundaries on you because you've taken advantage of me, and it stops right now!" My plan is simple. When something comes up and I feel I'm being used or taken for granted, I will use my tactics in Chapter 27, which sound nice but are direct. My boundaries will be set according to situations, I will stay vigilant and not backpedal, and eventually they will get the message.

Life is too short, and you can't afford to associate with those who bring you down. God wants us to love, be loved, have peace and joy, and live a clean and wholesome life. Unfortunately, we are not all equally yoked, and you will encounter people who are toxic. Your real friends will not treat you badly. You can be yourself around them with no fear of criticism, manipulation, and deception because they are not "poisonous" to you. But the sad news is that sometimes your friends will treat you better than your own family.

It's easy to walk away from someone who you thought was a friend, but to walk away from a family member is hurtful and difficult. I know because I had to do it. But in Matthew 10:14 it says, "If anyone will not welcome you or listen to your words, leave that home or town and shake the dust off your feet." Sometimes you have to walk away rather than let toxic people hurt you. Even though they're family, it doesn't mean that they're going to treat you well and are not capable of emotional or physical abuse. Many times our friends are more of a family than our own blood relatives. Even Jesus had to leave the place of his birth to perform miracles because his own town didn't believe in him.

Here is my prayer for you: I wish you happiness, peace, and joy. I pray that my books will be helpful to those who are desperately seeking a life that is filled with the love they deserve. May God bless you and keep you safe until you become the victor instead of the victim. In Jesus' name I pray...Amen.

PART IV

MY PORCH LIGHT

*EMBRACING A NEW CHAPTER
& THE ROAD TO RECOVERY*

Chapter 35

BE STILL AND KNOW

Well my friends, this is the final book of *The Porch Series*. It's been difficult and painful for me to tell my story about living with a sex addict, but God has gently led me through it every step of the way. I give him all the glory. He taught me how it *really* feels to walk by faith and not by sight.

I've been getting closer to God through writing these books and feel a presence like never before. Some days I cry tears of joy when I realize how much He loves me. I don't believe I've ever been as grateful as I am right now.

I've always been good about praying before I go to sleep, but now I find myself thanking him throughout the day for the small things I never paid attention to. My prayers were usually about asking for His help, but now I find myself asking how I can serve Him. I still end my prayers with "in Jesus' name, amen," but now I've added "thy will be done."

Looking back through my life, I realize I paid little attention to God when life was going well, but I turned to Him when things were bad. It took me *sixty-seven years* to discover that was not the type of relationship He desires. He wants a deep, intimate relationship with me, and it feels so good to know I'm never alone even though I live by myself. He's quickly becoming the best friend I've ever had because His love is unconditional. People can be fickle, but God's love never changes.

I'll never know all the things He's done for me in my lifetime, but there's no way I could have gotten to where I'm at right now by myself. In *Get off My Porch* and *Sitting on the Porch Swing*, I talked a lot about having PTSD and how difficult it was to deal with. I was running around in circles afraid that I couldn't get a handle on it, but now I'm not afraid because I know He'll be there to get me through.

PART IV: MY PORCH LIGHT

I still run into health issues because of my immune system being compromised, but I have a better attitude because *I know* He's the one who pulled me through when I was headed for anaphylactic shock twice. And above all, He's the author and the finisher of my life, and He'll decide when it's time for me to come home. So, it's all good! All I have to remember is "be still and know."

It's apparent that Frank is developing a stronger relationship with God as well. He's getting more involved with his Christian friends and has a desire to speak about his addiction, the consequences, the pain it's caused me, and his recovery plan. They say teaching is learning, so I believe this is a positive step in the right direction for him.

I have the daily devotional book by Sarah Young called *Jesus Calling* which helps me through my day. After Frank moved out, I loaned it to him hoping it would help. Evidently it did because he started calling me every day to read the devotion to *me*. I started missing my book, so he purchased his own. Now we discuss it daily. I'm careful to not push him, but sometimes it's the small things that can lead to big victories. I believe this is one of them.

Things have been going extremely well for quite a while. I'm starting to see just a tiny sliver of hope for our future, but I still don't trust the addict in him. We're both aware that if he doesn't regain my trust, this marriage will not survive.

The weather has changed since I finished the last part, and it's now spring. Frank has been coming over to help remodel the rock garden, and we've enjoyed our time outside. He's been patient and kind, and he seems to be eager to attend to my needs. He's always been a good helpmate, but everything was a serious project. Now he actually seems to enjoy helping.

We're both settled into our own homes now, and he still respects the boundaries I've set. I'm enjoying my crafts again, and the piano is starting to look quite inviting, But for some reason I'm still avoiding it. Like I said in *Sitting on the Porch*

Swing, starting is the hardest part, but once you get into it, you may have some fun and be distracted from your problems. I guess it's time for me to take my own advice, right?

Frank's starting to think more about what I may want or need instead of being selfish, and that's a *huge* step in the right direction for an addict. He knows how much I love the theater. I didn't know it, but *The Phantom of the Opera* is at the Fox Theatre in St. Louis, and he surprised me and asked if I wanted to go. Believe me, the tickets are expensive, but he didn't care. Now we're going to the theater!

I have to give credit where it's due. He's working hard to be the man God created and the husband I deserve. If he stays on his program with the determination I've witnessed, he may actually find the real Frank and kick the addict to the curb. He said he feels so much better about himself, and that's an area where I can encourage him.

We've discovered through trial and error that we can support each other in some ways, but we have to undo the psychological damage ourselves because we can't get into each other's minds (and trust me, I wouldn't want to see the mind of an addict). But the most important thing we've learned is to step back and let each other handle their own extreme emotions when they occur.

Now it's time for me to brag about *my* progress. *I have made the decision to not be a victim anymore.* I finally realized that I have the right to make my own choices about how my story will end. I *will not* allow anyone or anything to control my life again except God. I'm standing tall and taking my control back because God did not create me to be abused.

Being a victim is a miserable existence. It can take you down so hard that you lose all hope, but when you lose your faith, you're in trouble. I had lost my faith—not in God, but in my husband. But when I finally realized Frank wasn't strong enough to fight the addict himself without professional help, it changed everything. And I also knew I couldn't do it without counseling either. Now he has to fight his war, and I've been forced to fight a war I didn't ask for.

At this point, we're both determined to move forward and avoid the things that could set us back. We've had some bad moments but are getting better at resolving issues with less conflict, so that's progress. I'm impressed with that because in the past it was always his way or he'd verbally beat me down till I agreed. But I assure you, that *will never* happen again. Compromise is the key to resolving issues, and no one should have total control.

Chapter 36

THE LIGHT

Small children seem to have a natural fear of the darkness. It can be scary because of the monsters in the closet and under the bed, but when the light is turned on and they're comforted, the fear goes away.

I felt *My Porch Light* was an appropriate title for this book because when a visitor comes to my home at night, I turn on my porch light to see who it is. Once that person is in the light, I'll know if it's safe to let them in.

Addicts hide in their secret dark world of shame, guilt, and misery. They may think if they come out of the darkness and admit their addiction, it could be seen as a sign of weakness. Fear of being judged by others may also stop them from seeking help. Addicts live in an environment of dangerous denial, which is not only damaging to them but also to their partner.

But the light I'm referring to is sobriety—a clean, bright life with a spiritual connection to a higher power. Our higher power is God, and Frank knows beyond a shadow of a doubt that he will not be welcome in my life again as my husband unless he steps into that light and stays there.

I don't consider myself a prude, and I'm not so naïve that I don't know men objectify women and look at inappropriate material like pornography. But I do have my opinion. It's wrong, it's disgusting, and it's destroying relationships. It's like the Devil's stealing our men, and they're allowing it because they're too weak to stand up and do what's right. The secular world has them believing that you're not a man unless you participate in this sinful activity. But to me, that's not a man.

A real man is one who values his wife and children (if he has any) and treats them as a gift from God. A real man will not lower himself and be seduced by the filth which could destroy the woman he professes to love. A real man will not take the chance of leaving his children fatherless because he feels he's entitled due to the misconception "all men do it." A real man will not force his wife to compare herself to other women who she can't possibly compete with. And a real man has integrity, but a sex addict doesn't even begin to fall into that category.

I really get an attitude when I talk about this stuff! At the risk of sounding conceited, Frank hit the jackpot when he found me. I'm a woman who loves God and believes in the sanctity of marriage. To hear him describe me, I'm a regular girl scout. But the addict in him has brought out the wildcat in me. I didn't know I could be so hateful, and I get ashamed of myself when I allow him to push me that far. God must think I've changed my name to "Please Forgive Me."

Frank is not what I consider a "real man" yet. He has a long road ahead of him to regain my trust. Because nothing I said or did mattered and he didn't care how much pain he instilled on me, now he's paying the consequences and living alone. But my consequences of staying with him too long are much more severe.

I'll never understand how an addict can destroy the person they love with no regret or emotion. It's like their heart freezes and they feel nothing. I couldn't live with myself if I did that to someone. I would have been better off if he'd physically beat me because bruises heal, but he destroyed my self-worth, which will take a long time to heal.

You may have already suspected that I'm not having a good day by what I've written so far in this chapter, and you're right—I'm *very* angry and discouraged right now. I promised to take you through our recovery process, so I'm not going to hold back.

As I've said before, this last book will be written according to the ups and downs of our recovery. I may not write for months, or it could be several days in a row. Some days are good, some are fair, and some are bad. This is a bad one!

I'm dealing with PTSD again, but this time it's complicated. I'm not sure how to handle it. I feel like everything in my mind is frozen in a block of ice, and I can't get to the many emotions and flashbacks that have hit me pretty much back-to-back in the past week. I can't work on any particular thing because they're all bunched up, and I'm having trouble sorting things out. Today is a sad day for me because I discovered that the research has been much easier than actually applying the knowledge. I'm discouraged and emotional. But I did talk myself down from a panic attack, so that's a good start I suppose.

Frank's been asked to stay away for a while so I can work through this big pile of rubble. I discovered with the first PTSD episode that his presence brings out extreme anger in me because I know he's responsible for my condition. He tries to help and is sweet, but I get angry and lash out at him at the drop of a hat.

About a week ago, a friend of mine whose husband is an addict called to talk. She just recently found out that he was viewing pornography again and was really upset. I listened and tried to give her comfort, but it brought back some terrible memories for me when she went through the events. He'd been out of town for some time and was heading home, and she didn't know if she could even be around him.

This conversation took me back to the time when I discovered Frank was also into pornography, and I couldn't stop dozens of incidents from the past from running through my mind. Then she talked about how it hurt her so bad and how she was in a deep depression. To top it all off, she talked in detail about how it made her feel as a woman and her struggle with a poor body image. I've been working so hard on that one, and suddenly I felt old, fat, and undesirable again.

I did my best to help during her countless calls, but with PTSD it's miserable because you relive events just like they're happening all over again. I didn't think it would affect me, but it certainly did. Frank noticed the change in me and suggested that maybe I wasn't ready to talk to her about it, so he called and told her it was having a big effect on me. She was understanding, but the damage was done. I don't blame her at all because I made myself available and didn't realize I wasn't ready to handle a situation like that yet. Of course, then I felt guilty for not being available for her when she was in trouble.

The next incident happened at a social function. I dressed up and thought I looked pretty cute, but after we got there, some eye candy walked in. This woman had all the right equipment and was quite young. Some addicts tend to be drawn to a specific body build, and this chick had it. I know the type of woman that catches his eye because I've watched him do it since we've been married. Of course, now my mind goes to the *hundreds* of incidents when I watched him objectify women, and that added to my trauma.

And of course my mother had to put in her two cents worth by giving my little sister a hard time, so that took me back to all the emotional abuse she's caused me. If you put them all together, it equals a mountain of stress and anxiety. This all happened within a week. Sometimes I don't think this marriage is even worth fighting for and that I'd be better off single. On the other hand, Frank's been sweet to me, but unfortunately I'm mad at him all over again.

Well, obviously I have a lot of work to do and am not looking forward to it. I guess I need to read through all my research again to figure out how to sort this out. Frank just texted to check on me and said he's going to do a lot of praying right now, which I really could use! The first PTSD episode took four days to get past and the second one lasted three days, so maybe I'll get lucky and clear up this mess in two.

Chapter 37

THE FALLEN PRINCESS

I've always believed in God and have wondered many times throughout my life what Heaven is like. I figured since Christ is King, I must be a princess! But I don't feel like one today. My dreams of "happily ever after" have been shattered three times now. I married my first husband twice and thought for sure it would work the second time, but I just couldn't stay with him. I did everything I could to make the marriage work, but we weren't equally yoked and had different beliefs.

When I married Frank I thought he was the answer to my prayers for a good Christian man. He attended church regularly, knew the Bible well, and seemed to have good morals. But little did I know there was an evil entity deep within him—an addict—and it's a vicious creature that will stop at nothing to have control and destroy the man within. Unfortunately, I know the addict better than I know the man who's trapped inside.

Today I'm absolutely exhausted from trying to stay in this horrific game of trying to find Frank. How can I possibly do that when I'm dealing with my own issues from PTSD? Even if I decide not to stay in the marriage, I know I still have to repair the emotional damage it's caused in order to move forward with my life and have peace. I've always considered myself to be a strong woman, but today I feel like a lost little girl.

I've been thinking about my childhood a lot this morning. I was a happy little girl with two brothers and one sister (my dear younger sister was born ten years after I was). We were a good close family, and life was great. After high school, I immediately went to work as a secretary and started my adult life. There were ups and downs and the usual "traumatic" events (that seem so trivial now), but I was a happy camper.

PART IV: MY PORCH LIGHT

Then I got married, and my whole life started to change—and not in a good way. I have two wonderful sons who are the loves of my life, and they're the only reason I made it through being married to their dad twice. My sons were adults when I divorced him the second time and had left home to start their own lives. I rented a little doll house that became my sanctuary. I was forty-six years old and had finally found the peace I so desperately needed.

Then along came Frank, and the chaos started all over again. But Cat the Optimist stayed with him nineteen years before I finally had enough and asked him to leave. But during the marriage to Frank, I was blessed with a wonderful daughter-in-law and three gorgeous granddaughters. The love of my children and grandchildren kept me going, while Frank took me down. So here I sit alone again at age sixty-seven with no children to raise and back to square one. I know God is watching over me, but I'm upset with myself for allowing two men to steal my youth and happiness.

Out of curiosity, I made a list of the women I personally know who say they will *never* get married again and was astonished at how many there were (I'm a social butterfly and know a lot of people.) I broke them down into categories and found out there were six who are divorced, five widows, and eight who are married but extremely unhappy. That's a total of eighteen women who will be living by themselves for the rest of their lives. There are just two on the list who are willing to date but not commit. Three of the widows had great husbands but believe they'll never find that kind of man again. And if I don't stay married to Frank, I will indeed join this group of women because life is getting shorter and I don't intend to spend it being unhappy.

That's just *my* list, and I think it's disgraceful! I know for a fact that the biggest majority of these women were not treated well, and six of them had to deal with pornography. The women are fleeing, but the men usually continue to shop around for a replacement...and the Devil is smiling.

The women I listed are good women, but I'm not going to excuse the women who also contribute to failed relationships. They take advantage of men and throw them away like yesterday's newspaper if they don't get what they want from them. These women don't mind being involved with a married man and holding them for ransom. They enjoy the attention and gifts but tend to forget there's an unhappy wife and possibly children involved who will be destroyed should the secret of their affair be exposed.

I have to admit I seriously thought about having an affair with a single man and had the chance, but I couldn't bring myself to do it. The reason I was so tempted was because I was receiving little intimacy in the bedroom with Frank and felt like I was just being used as a maid. I felt totally abandoned, and that's a terrible and dangerous place for anyone to be. But God slapped me around a bit, and I came to my senses.

Sexual addicts are so busy chasing fantasies they can never have, and the family suffers. Their partner is basically ignored unless the addict has a need for them, and the children (especially the same sex children) have no moral compass and live in a dysfunctional atmosphere. Husbands are supposed to be the spiritual leaders of the family, but they're more interested in what they *can't have* than what's standing right before them.

My positive male role model was my dad. He died in 1998, and I miss him every day. He was an amazing man and a great example of how a father loves their children. It didn't matter what the problem was—Dad had the solution. He spent time with his children, and we never questioned his love for us. Watching him struggle with congestive heart failure was painful. Even on his deathbed he smiled, and those beautiful brown eyes still displayed his love. He couldn't speak because of all the tubes but could write. Before I left his room for the last time, he wrote "See you later" on a napkin. He died that night, and a piece of my heart died with him.

PART IV: MY PORCH LIGHT

My brother Dave was another positive male role model in my life. We were best friends, and he was my "go to" guy. Even though he lived in Alabama, when he came home, he always set aside a day to spend with me. He survived for many years after his plane crash, but he died in 2005.

The last man standing in our family unit is my brother Larry who lives in California. I get to see him two or three times a year. "Lightning Larry" is a well-known sharp shooter and karate expert and owns a successful security business. We're pretty close, but I don't get to see him as often as I'd like to.

Right now, I don't feel like anybody's princess, and I miss it. I can hold onto memories of my dad and brother and occasionally see my brother from California, but it's not the same. I hope someday I can be Frank's princess, but if not, I'll still be a princess in God's eyes.

Chapter 38

THE UNWELCOMED GUEST

Frank's been gone now for five months. We've been seeing each other pretty much every day, and things had been going extremely well. He was being thoughtful, caring, and attentive, and it appeared he was making excellent progress. But the relationship is now in a downward spiral and spinning out of control. I'm right on the edge of stopping the madness and moving on.

I've been feeling unsettled for about a month now and couldn't figure out why. When he came over, I wasn't comfortable around him most of the time and felt relieved when he left. Don't get me wrong, he was still being nice and sweet to me, but I felt something was seriously wrong. At first I thought it was just me getting too used to my independence, but then it became apparent that he was slowly trying to gain control of me again.

I've talked a lot about "gaslighting" in my previous books, and he's definitely *attempting* to use it on me again. He tends to forget that I've been researching sexual addiction for over six months and have written books on the subject. I know *exactly* what he's doing, and he's *not going to get by with it*. I recently started calling him out on his behavior, and of course he's telling lies to cover up other lies, which are typical behaviors of an addict. Little does he know he's digging a deep hole for himself that he won't be able to climb out of, and if he gets out of the hole, he may discover that his wife is gone.

I've really been looking forward to going to the theater, but two days ago I found out that he's been lying to me since last October about his sobriety. I'm not in the habit of asking about it because he lets me know all the time that he's "clean" and has been since leaving treatment. But for some reason, I felt the need to ask that fatal question and totally caught him off-guard. His initial response was total silence for a short time, and I knew.

He fessed up and said he had acted out twice since he came back from counseling and felt it was important for me to understand what led him to do it. I told him I didn't want to hear it, but he insisted. He said, "The first time was..." and told me about his failure but blamed it on *me*. At the time I was out-of-state with my cousin and ended up in the hospital because I had a severe breakout due to my weak immune system, and *he* felt guilty for the way he had mistreated me over the years. But then he acted like the conversation was over.

This is a perfect example of gaslighting, and I knew immediately what he was doing. He was trying to make me believe it was *my* fault and if I hadn't ended up in the hospital *he* would have been fine. Of course, his goal was to become a victim of circumstances, and I was supposed to feel sorry for him because he would never have failed if it wasn't for me. It wasn't bad enough that I went into anaphylactic shock and got there just in time; I must also feel bad that I was the cause of ruining his perfectly clean record (yeah, right).

He changed the subject, and we discussed some issues I had around his behavior. Then he got a phone call from his buddy and said, "Gotta go." I let him know that I didn't appreciate his quick departure because I was in the middle of talking about something that was important to me. He apologized and offered to stay, but I politely reminded him where the door was several times before he left.

That night I remembered he didn't tell me about the second episode, so I asked him about it the next day. He lied and said he didn't say there were two and commenced to defend himself. When I reminded him that he looked me right in the face when he told me, he said we were talking on the phone when the conversation took place.

Of course being the good little Christian girl that I am, I went off on him (and yes, I had to ask forgiveness for my cursing), but I *did not back down!* In the past, I would have given in and said he was right in order to stop an argument because I hate any kind of dissension. That's how he used to control me, beating me down emotionally with his lies to defend himself, but that's not going to work anymore.

His goal was to make me believe I was so stupid that I didn't even remember where I was when he made a confession that negated all the progress I thought we'd made. He implied that I imagined looking into the dark and sinful eyes of an addict who was gaslighting me so I would feel responsible for his failure. I knew what was going on and watched his performance, which was disturbing because in his twisted mind he still believes he can get me back in line and control me.

At that point, I knew I was dealing with the addict, not the Godly man I know Frank has the ability to be. But the good news is I'm not afraid of being emotionally abused anymore because I know what's going on. I'm not going to waste my time arguing with the evil entity that resides in my husband's mind. So now the addict in Frank has become an unwelcomed guest in my home. It was time to set another boundary.

If Frank is here and I see *just one addictive behavior*, he will be asked to leave. Since he's not a violent man, I have no fear of physical abuse. So far he's been cooperative and respects the previous boundaries I've set. Now that I've discovered he's getting weak and is allowing the addict to take control sometimes, I have to hold my own and let him know there will be absolutely no chance of reconciliation until he conquers his addiction and wants to live a clean and healthy life the way God intended. And then he has to prove it to me, which will not be an easy task. He has to decide what he's willing to give up or lose. So now the ball's in his court.

Frank's last performance destroyed all the excitement I had about going to the theater, and now I refuse to go because he'll ruin it for me if he starts objectifying women. It's like taking an unruly child to Walmart—you have to make sure they don't break anything, but in my case it would be my heart because he had me believing he was clean. My friend and her husband will enjoy the three-hundred-dollar tickets, and Frank will just have to take the financial loss. Addicts are well-known for this behavior. They will do nice things for you out of guilt, so it's hard to tell when it comes from their heart.

But there's more to his deception because I haven't been the only one he's betrayed. He has a weekly group meeting with the guys he was in counseling with and admitted that he's lied to them as well. He's led them to believe he's been "holier than thou clean" and that we're doing fantastic. I called him out on it while I was on my rampage, and he's promised that he'll confess his deception in the next meeting. He said he's already told one of the guys and would be willing to give me his phone number to confirm it, but I'm not going to call.

Frank's arrogance is over the top, and he has a need to be the smartest and most advanced in anything he does. Through his lies, he's convinced the group that he has all the answers and is starting to believe he can actually counsel people himself. The only reason things have been going well for him is because he has a wife who took the initiative to study his addiction. He needs to realize that he's not in control anymore and, unless God has other plans, he may end up alone with his best friend—the addict.

The day after the blowup Frank was so desperate to prove that he finally "saw the light" that he reached into his bag of tricks and played the God card. That surprised me because evidently he doesn't remember that stopped working years ago. I used to fall for that trick, but when it became apparent he was using God to manipulate me, I made quite a scene. The least he could have done was be creative and come up with something I hadn't seen before!

He sent text after text celebrating his deliverance from sin. God had gotten ahold of him and straightened him out. He even called John Hagee Ministries and got saved over the phone! He was done being an addict, and his destructive behavior was stopping *right now*! He started quoting scripture and was going to walk in the light of God forever! God had taken over, and he was a new man!

Needless to say, I wasn't excited and didn't share in his enthusiasm because I knew what the outcome would be. He's gone down this road probably a hundred times in the nineteen years we've been married. He's a praying man who will give his problem to God and ask for help, but he immediately takes it back (sometimes the next day) because he thinks he's "got it now" and can do it himself. I believe his intentions are good, but he's not able to sustain them. That's the narcissist coming out in him. He obviously thinks he's smarter than God.

The next day when we were talking on the phone he confessed that he hadn't been taking good care of his personal hygiene (he's always been a clean guy, and I had already picked up on that one), wasn't able to sleep, was eating poorly, and wasn't taking his supplements. He talked so fast and loud that it was obvious his emotions were out of control. He claimed that his memory wasn't good either, but that one didn't fly with me because he's used that a lot over the years to avoid telling the truth.

I'd known for a couple of months that he was starting to revert back to some of his old habits. I pointed it out to him several times, and of course he came up with excuses of being tired or overwhelmed with projects he was working on. I didn't expect him to own it, but I gave it a shot.

The first thing I noticed was that he stopped listening to me about general everyday conversations and basically blew me off. I had to start asking him if he heard what I said, to which he usually said yes, but when I questioned him about it, he had no idea. This may sound petty on my part, but I call that lying. Before we separated, that had been a huge problem because what I had to say didn't matter to him—it was all about what he wanted.

After we separated, he would act like he was glad to see me and needed hugs and kisses, but now he walks in like he lives here and basically ignores me intimately (not sexually because that's been off limits since he got back from treatment). When that started, I got suspicious about his sobriety, and that's when I caught him off guard and asked him about it.

First he admitted when he had fallen down once, when I reminded him that he said it was two times, he said it was twice but that was all. I don't believe it for a minute because an addict will *never* admit to all their setbacks. It's just like the alcoholic who says they've only had two drinks, which usually means six.

I finally told him that his emotions were out of control, he was heading in a bad direction, and I thought he needed private counseling. To my surprise, he agreed and left a message with his counselor in Colorado to start private phone sessions. Then he confessed that he hadn't been working his program like he should and agreed with me when I said we were spending too much time together.

So here's my plan, and I've made it very clear to him. He won't be allowed to come over daily and just hang out. I'm going to happy-up, enjoy my day, and get back to my peaceful life. His behavior has been bringing me down and affecting my recovery, and it stops right now. I have decided to see him just two or three times a week, and that time won't be wasted hanging around my house, eating dinner, watching television, and acting like the miserable married couple we were. He's gotten way too comfortable here, but I have to take part of the blame for allowing him to come over so much.

I told him it's time to go back to square one and date me because I need to find out if I have any intimate feelings for him now. He needs to know what it feels like to not have me around every day and find out if he will even miss me. We may both be done with the marriage and not even realize it. He reluctantly agreed, but I think it's a good idea. I'm willing to give it a shot because he was doing so well and was really proud of himself, and I was starting to feel closer to him. Somewhere along the way he fell down, and now he's so ashamed of himself that he's willing to do anything to make things right. But I'm getting tired of the uncertainty of what my future will be.

He's been an addict for over thirty-five years but expected to conquer it in just a few months. I think he now understands this isn't a quick fix and is going to take a lot of work, patience, and time. But the biggest lesson he's taken away from this setback is that he can't do it alone and seriously needs to humble himself and stay close to God. He allowed the narcissist to take charge, and down he went!

PART IV: MY PORCH LIGHT

Chapter 39

TIME TO GET REAL

I've always been a caring person who loves deeply and takes my relationships seriously. If someone I care about is ill or has a personal problem, I check on them, sometimes daily depending on the situation. They may need something from the store, a babysitter, or maybe just someone to listen. I know what it's like to feel helpless, and I always appreciate those who care enough to take time out of their day to check on me.

When Frank and I separated, we contacted the special people in our life to let them know what was going on. At first we told them about his control and manipulation, which was true because that's the behavior of an addict, but we waited for a period of time before we told them about the addiction. I was the one who demanded the separation because I couldn't stand to even look at him, let alone live under the same roof.

Since then, I've heard rumors flying around about why Cat "threw" him out. They included such things as: "She pitched him out because she's spoiled and didn't get her way about something," "She's so selfish—it's all about her," "She has everything, but it's never enough." Here's the truth: I gave him a choice between divorce and separation because I had been living with a disgusting, controlling, and manipulative filthy sex addict!

As far as being spoiled, selfish, and having everything, let's talk about my *perfect private life* with Frank shall we? I'm going to be sixty-eight years old in a few weeks, and here's what I have: I live in a nice home, drive a nice car, am secure financially, and have "stuff." However, my husband is a sex addict and a lot of the nice "stuff" was given to me out of guilt because he emotionally abused me, lied, manipulated, and totally ignored my intimate needs.

So here I sit writing this book, living alone (even though I have a husband), trying to put myself back together emotionally, and scared to death that someday my immune system will bottom out again if I don't control my stress and stay calm. Material items mean *nothing* if you don't have peace and feel loved. People who haven't had to deal with trauma like this are quick to judge, but maybe they need to sweep the dirt off their own front porch before they start on mine because they obviously don't know anything about unconditional love.

Since Frank has moved out, these same people have never checked on me to see how I'm doing or if I might need emotional support. They avoid me like the plague and change the subject when I try to talk to them about my situation. And I know for a fact that my mother is right in the middle of this massacre. These people are some of the ones who I've always tried to be there for and thought I could depend on through this tough time, but I was wrong.

Everything's changed now, so they'll need to call on someone else. It's been really painful to discover *they're* the selfish ones and have been using me. I was there for them unconditionally, but when I was the one who needed support and encouragement, they deserted me. It's all been one-sided. I started feeling like a fool, but I had to remind myself that God knows my heart and understands why I won't put myself in that position again.

I won't sever relationships because I do love them, and I'm the one who's allowed them to take advantage of me. I had to learn the hard way, but I'm still blessed with the ones who truly care and are there for me. Unfortunately, the majority of them are my friends—not my family—and it broke my heart to admit it.

But I'm happy to say my younger sister whom Mom tried to take away from me is my biggest supporter. She truly understands my situation because that's the reason she divorced her husband. She makes an effort to contact me, is willing to listen, and I know she's there for me unconditionally as I am with her. Now *that's* the way we were raised, and I'm glad we both held on to that valuable lesson.

During the time I was telling my friends about his addiction, I was surprised to find out that several of them had divorced their husband for the same reason but never admitted it because it was degrading and embarrassing. I thought about the help they could have received from counseling and felt sorry for them because they all loved their husbands but now are alone and will probably never trust another man again.

Sexual addiction is by far the biggest monster in the closet. However, it does exist and is becoming an epidemic. People talk freely about other addicts, such as alcoholics, overeaters, shopaholics, gamblers, kleptomaniacs, hypochondriacs, and technology addicts, but sex addicts are off-limits. I'm not defending them by any means—I'm just being real.

Every couple dealing with sexual addiction will have different circumstances, so the destruction will vary according to the situation. But keep in mind sexual addiction is not just a man's disorder. I was surprised to learn that women can also become sex addicts due to lack of intimacy, poor body image, and feeling unloved. Of course, there are other reasons, but I won't go into those. The following is just a short list of the some of the consequences of sexual addiction:

- Loss of intimacy

- Divorce

- Financial difficulties

- Fatherless/Motherless children

- Loss of integrity

- Low self-esteem/Poor body image

- Suicidal attempts

- Isolation

- Stress/Depression/Anger/Guilt

- Loss of job

- Feeling unworthy

- Obsessive behavior

- Denial

I could fill three pages with the damages *any* addiction can cause. Here's a list of a few addictions that includes a short list of the behaviors and consequences of each.

Alcoholics: They can be physically, verbally, and emotionally abusive, neglectful, and illogical, and they could have no recollection of their behavior. They may risk the safety of themselves as well as others, start physical fights that could lead to assault, kill someone while driving drunk, possibly rape someone, and drain finances.

The consequences could be health problems, loss of family, loss of job, depression, anger, guilt, loss of integrity, criminal record, suicide, financial ruin, and loss of libido.

Overeaters: Some of the behaviors of overeaters may include eating large quantities of food when not hungry, eating in secret, hiding food, eating quickly, obsessive eating, denial about eating habits, and a variety of excuses for their weight gain.

The consequences could be low self-esteem, withdrawal from family and friends, difficulty dealing with stress, anger, sensitivity about body shape, shame and guilt around food, bloated abdomen, weight gain, and health problems.

Shopaholics: The behaviors of a shopaholic may be overspending, compulsive purchases, chronic shopping, lying about money, purchasing items on credit if they don't have cash, obsession around money, and shopping to heal pain.

The consequences could be bankruptcy, shame, guilt, depression, hopelessness, anger, unworthiness, and excessive stress.

Gamblers: The behaviors of a compulsive gambler may be failure to control your gambling, feeling guilty after a loss, taking bigger risks and spending more money to recoup a loss, borrowing money to gamble, neglecting financial responsibilities, selling possessions or taking out a loan to gamble, and avoiding work or social commitments.

The consequences of gambling may be financial ruin (loss of house, car, job, personal possessions, etc.), loss of relationships and friends, stress, anger, shame, guilt, and bankruptcy.

Kleptomaniacs: Some of the behaviors are urges to steal unneeded items, thoughts of intrusion, struggling with mood disorders, inability to resist compulsion to steal, release of pressure following theft, getting pleasure or gratification after theft, and increased stress that leads to theft.

These consequences can be devastating. The addict will be seen as a thief, they can get arrested and incarcerated, and their family and friends may pull away because they don't trust them. They may lose their job, have a criminal record, and develop a poor self-image that could possibly lead to drug abuse. Remorse, guilt, shame, anger, and stress can lead to dangerous behavior.

Hypochondriacs: These addicts have a habit of frequently changing doctors and checking their vital signs. They are not reassured by an examination, constantly fear that they may have a serious debilitating disease, and frequently check the body for lumps, sores, muscles aches, or anything that may appear suspicious. Minor symptoms may be seen as the onset of a deadly disease, which creates extreme stress for them.

The consequences of being a hypochondriac can get ugly because they can literally make themselves sick, which could lead to a serious illness.

Technology addicts: Some behaviors of technology addictions can be isolation, lack of performing routine tasks, procrastination, no sense of time, inability to prioritize, anxiety, dishonesty, avoidance of people, mood swings, agitation, and feelings of euphoria when using the device.

Consequences can be neck pain, headaches, insomnia, dry eyes, poor hygiene, carpal tunnel, failure to eat or excessive eating with no exercise, backache, and stress. I believe this addiction is becoming more common!

Okay readers, here's what I'd like for you to do now. Go back to the list of consequences of a sex addict and read it again. You'll find *each and every* consequence somewhere in the above addictions.

I think the reason sexual addiction is not openly discussed is because the word "sex" is connected to it, which really confuses me because you can't get away from it! It's acceptable in movies, commercials, children's cartoons, billboards, magazines, and so much more. Teenagers are being encouraged to take birth control "just in case," and I believe that gives them permission to *have* sex. They are allowed to go out in public with too much of their private stuff on display, and their parents allow it so they will be "accepted."

Children are being raised in this environment, and it's time to get real, be honest, stand up, and fight *all* addictions. People have absolutely no problem saying the word "sex," and pornography is becoming acceptable (although it's destroying marriages and relationships). But you can't connect it to the word "addiction"? You could be raising a sex addict *right now* if you don't monitor what they watch, the websites they're viewing, and who they're spending time with.

It's parents' jobs to teach these precious children how to become responsible adults. God's plan for blessing us with children *does not* include ignoring them and setting them up for failure. If you don't get off your behind, pay attention, and sacrifice your time to monitor their activities and teach them good morals, they could end up living a miserable life.

If you have children, I want you to take a second, close your eyes, and see their beautiful faces. Are they worth the sacrifice of your time? Do you want them to be happy? Do you love them unconditionally, or are they obstacles in your busy life? Keep in mind, addiction can be the end result of internal emotional pain, and if children don't get the time and guidance they deserve with their parents, they will *definitely* go to someone else for attention, which could be the biggest mistake of their life.

If your child gets married and has children of their own, they will more than likely use the techniques that you did, which could be a good thing if you've done it correctly. But if not, it could become a generational curse, and the children will continue to suffer the consequences.

I wasn't a perfect parent and don't believe anyone can be, but I did my best to teach my sons good morals, manners, and how to love. Today, they are not only my sons but my friends, and I love them as much as I did when they were little boys. Yes, I got tired and some nights I didn't lay down to sleep, I literally fell into bed exhausted, but they were my responsibility. It was my job to prepare them for adulthood.

Some people are like cattle, just following the herd now with no thought about where they're going to end up. You don't need to fit in with that crowd. Stand up, be an example, and help turn things back around. Your children are worth it.

Chapter 40

D-DAY

Frank and I had been scooting along okay, but somewhere along the way I started to feel uncomfortable, disrespected, and unloved again. I think it may have started after he lied about his sobriety, and I couldn't seem to get that out of my mind. I really wanted to believe that he's made progress, but the past had been haunting me. I'm aware that it was PTSD, but I was seriously struggling to get past his most current deception.

I wasn't comfortable around him most of the time anymore, and I was just waiting for another lie to surface. It's all about trust, which was the main obstacle for me, and I couldn't move forward if he wouldn't stop lying to me. I told him that we all know when we're lying, and most of the time it's premeditated. He agreed but obviously believed he could still get by with it since it's *just* guilt by omission and I'm such a forgiving person. I know most addicts are habitual liars, but he had almost nine months to get control of it. This was not going to work for me anymore. It was time to pull the trigger.

In June, we signed papers for an uncontested divorce. I couldn't be involved in this ungodly union anymore—it just felt wrong to me, even though I'm innocent. I hired the lawyer, and we went together to sign the documents. Then we had lunch and talked a little bit about things. It was a numbing experience, and I'm slowly beginning to accept the reality that he forced me into making the decision by continuing to lie.

I'm not angry anymore, but I'm hurt and disappointed because it appears he believes he still has some type of control over me. I have to admit I allowed that control, but I've warned him too many times that if I divorced him, it would most likely be the lying that pushed me over the edge. He obviously didn't believe me. He has only himself to blame, but I have no guilt—I kept my vows through better or worse.

My birthday was in June as well. Frank came over with flowers and a card in hand and then offered to get my mail. When he came back to the house he had a sorrowful look on his face. I saw the large envelope in his hand and knew it was the finalized divorce papers. He knew it would be in my mailbox because he got his papers that day too. Well, happy birthday Cat! It was a sad moment, but we talked and worked through the emotions before company showed up for the celebration.

Frank made my birthday special, and I had a great time even though the reality of the divorce popped in and out of my mind throughout the evening. That was a pretty expensive birthday gift, right? It makes me wonder if God had a hand in this somehow. Receiving the finalized papers on my birthday may have been his way of saying happy "re-birth" to a new chapter of my life.

I know for a fact that I'm supposed to be serving God by helping other partners of sex addicts and sharing my knowledge, so maybe this was his way of giving me the freedom to do his will. That's the only thing that keeps me grounded right now because Frank simply doesn't respect me. But that's okay—God is more important than anything else in my life.

Since we started out as good friends before we dated, we have a mutual agreement to try and maintain that friendship. I know I can trust him as a friend but not as a lover. Of course he was upset when I told him I was filing for the divorce. He said he would take any type of relationship I was willing to give him to keep me in his life. I know I can depend on him for anything I may need (except for intimacy), and I know I could be there for him as well.

He asked to come over yesterday, and we played cards, ate dinner, and watched television. It was pretty amazing how comfortable I was around him since the pressure is gone. We both talked about the emotions we have around the divorce and then agreed that we would keep any negative feelings to ourselves from now on. We have people we can talk to if necessary, but to keep hashing it out would be detrimental to our plan of remaining friends.

I don't know if it's going to work, but I have always treasured his friendship. So, we'll see. It's sad that I couldn't trust him as a lover and that he broke my heart, but I do love him as a person. I just can't spend the rest of my life being on edge and allowing him to control my peace of mind, happiness, and future. Unless God has other plans, this is the best I could offer him. But to be truthful, I'm hoping we can make it as friends.

I started thinking about why I made the decision to divorce him because we'd been getting along quite well. He admitted to me a long time ago that he was having a hard time being honest because it had become habitual. Every time I caught him lying, I confronted him. He'd get so upset with himself and seemed desperate to be rid of that destructive part of the addiction. I began to feel like I'd bailed out on him and didn't keep my promise to support him in his recovery.

For the last few months I thought about ending the marriage every day and couldn't get it out of my mind. It didn't make sense because no matter what obstacle we encountered, we were able to work it out. I went out with my cousin for the evening last night and told her I felt guilty about deserting him, and she kind of rocked my world when she said, "He deserted *you*." Well, that brought me back to reality.

Since I have custody of our dog Miss Babette, Frank was staying with her while I was out because she's fourteen years old and has separation anxiety. When I got home, I told him about the discussion my cousin and I had, and he agreed he was indeed the culprit. We ended up talking about many things, and I suddenly realized that it wasn't *him* I divorced—*it was the addict*. It was quite an impactful moment. It's times like this that I know God's doing a work in us.

I'm sad for him because as I've said many times in my books, he's a good man. Life got messy for him before we met, and he medicated his pain with the addiction. I know the only heartache I may have in the future with him now is if we can't remain friends because I love him dearly. He's probably the best friend I've ever had, and I have a lot of good friends. He said last night that it made him feel good that I divorced the addict in him and not the person. When he left, it was obvious that a big weight had been lifted off him, and I felt *very* safe and relaxed. For us, the divorce was a good decision because there will be no sexual intimacy to worry about—hopefully we can just be friends.

I've really been working on my self-esteem and body image, and I'm feeling much better about myself. I don't believe I'm an old, fat, and ugly woman anymore, so that's a huge step in the right direction. I have mirrors and am finally able to see myself as a lovely and shapely mature woman who would be desirable to someone else. But I'm definitely not interested in *any* relationship at this point.

Right now, I'm content with being a mom, enjoying my grandchildren, and spending time with my friends. I'm in the process of learning a new craft and am excited about creating beautiful pieces. God gave me an awesome gift of creativity, so I'm not going to sit around and mope. And my friend the piano is still patiently waiting for me to return. I look at it every day now, but for some reason I'm just not ready yet. But once I start playing again, I may very well end up in jail for disturbing the peace because it's always been my biggest passion.

I'll keep you posted about how the friendship thing works for a few months. Please pray for us. Even though we couldn't make it as husband and wife, I believe God would be happy to see us be mature about the situation and still love each other because that's what he's all about—love.

I'd like to tell you about a dream I had years ago when I was extremely ill and had decided to stay with Frank until I died. I truly believed my death was coming soon, and since I couldn't handle the medical expenses and needed the insurance, I was in a bad position. This dream had such a huge effect on me, and it's as clear in my mind today as it was back then.

I'm looking down at a huge maze and see myself desperately running around, trying to find my way out. I keep turning corners only to discover there's a dead end in each one. I sit down, cry, then get back up and start running again. Suddenly I hear a voice in my dream that says "There goes Cat...She's running again...Now she's crying...She's up...No—she's down." Then another voice says, "Shall I go help her?" and the first voice says "No...let her go."

In my dream it appears that I'm physically exhausted, but I keep going. Finally, I sit in a corner and cry for a long time. All at once, I look up and stretch both my hands up, and I hear the first voice say "There's my girl."

I have my own interpretation of that dream. I was so emotionally torn up and ill that I didn't know which way to turn. No matter what I did, I found no relief. I believe the first voice was God, and the other one was an angel. God was just waiting for me to turn to him and ask for help. Remember, he's a gentleman and very patient.

Over the years, I've learned that God is always there, but we must humble ourselves and realize there are certain things in our life that we cannot control. We stress out, get angry, and give up. It seems like we only turn to him when we're desperate. I've discovered that when you totally commit to God and give him control, amazing things happen.

Now that I've put God first and want to please and serve him, life has gotten a lot easier. Even though we're divorced now, I know beyond a shadow of a doubt that he will never leave nor forsake me, and that gives me tremendous comfort. Yes, I still get stupid and run amok for a while, but I'm getting much better at catching myself and turning to God. I've spent a lot of years in the wastelands, but now I'm standing up and am claiming my right to be happy. I'm a child of God, and it doesn't get any better than that!

Chapter 41

TAKE IT SLOW—LET IT GO

I just got back from Colorado last week. My oldest granddaughter turned fifteen, and since she was born, I've been there to celebrate every one of her birthdays. She's a lovely young lady now, and it's hard to believe that all three of my precious granddaughters are growing up so quickly. Not to be partial, but I believe my granddaughters are the most beautiful creatures God ever made. I'm beginning to see their talents and dreams. The oldest wants to be an artist and is in fact quite talented in that field, and the middle one has a passion for animals and wants to be a veterinarian (which she will excel at). The youngest one is nine and isn't old enough to have an opinion yet, but I know with whatever she chooses, she'll strive to be the best.

Frank knows that the trip to Colorado each year is a given, and when I talked about looking for airline tickets, he asked if we would be going together. I said no. I know it hurt his feelings, but he's literally ruined every trip we've ever been on with his objectification of women and ignoring me. It was time to go solo and enjoy myself. I had the pleasure of meeting my future daughter-in-law, and she's precious. We hit it off immediately, and I know she's going to be a wonderful addition to the family. I had a wonderful time and desperately needed the break.

While preparing for her birthday party, their front patio needed to be swept. I love to work outside and volunteer. I started out with a broom before my son suggested that I use a leaf blower. Well, the leaf blower I had at home has two speeds—high and hurricane. It's a bulky and heavy contraption, and I had a bad experience the first and only time I used it. Let's just say I made a few people angry who were driving by because my leaves were hitting their windshields. I just about landed on my fanny and couldn't control it. But my son assured me that his was much lighter and that I would be able to use it. After I got back from my trip, I purchased one like his, so now I can blow my leaves without causing a scene.

While I was blowing the leaves on his patio, I had a revelation, which had a huge impact on me. I realized that I needed to "sweep" my mind and keep it clear and safe, just like the title for the last book. It's like walking on the patio barefoot and stepping on a rock, which could be painful. Just like leaves, dirt, and rocks don't belong on a porch or patio, negative thoughts and painful events of the past don't belong in my mind. Betrayal trauma has caused a lot of physical and emotional damage in my life, and I realized that I've *allowed* my mind to go back to bad memories that are huge triggers for PTSD.

Before I left for my trip, my son Mark and I enjoyed a breakfast together, and he said something so profound that I decided it would be the title of this chapter. He said, "Take it slow and let it go." That statement made me realize that I needed to slow down and tackle each bad thought or memory *as they happen* and let go of each one individually instead of attempting to destroy all my negative thoughts at once—which I've now discovered is virtually impossible! I've been putting them all in the same basket and trying to forget everything at once, which makes the task insurmountable. He has no idea how that one statement will help with my PTSD.

Here's how I plan to use that knowledge. Let's say, for instance, that an intrusive image or bad memory pops up. I'm going to stay focused on that *one thought* and not allow myself to start piling up similar incidents that will add to my anxiety. I will remember that the incident was in the past and *is not a current threat to me*—it's already happened, it's over, and it's just a bad memory. My goal is to clean up my mind and get rid of the past that's been causing me pain.

I realize this is going to take time, but I believe this is the most powerful tool I've ever run across—even with my research. It simply involves common sense and makes sense to me. The mind is powerful, and we must learn that we have the ability to control our minds. I've been running around in circles for too long, and it's time to step into my mind and give it the peace it so desperately needs.

If we allow people and bad memories to control our minds, we are doing a huge disservice to the beautiful minds that God gave us. As I put this new technique into practice, the addict will slowly curl up and die. Frank may choose to keep the addict, but Cat is taking it slow and letting it go as it shows up—right into the garbage with the other filth!

PART IV: MY PORCH LIGHT

Chapter 42

A YEAR AGO TODAY

Today is September 9, 2018. Frank went for counseling one year ago today. We have been separated for almost nine months now and divorced for three of those months, so I figured it was time for an update.

I just returned from another getaway with my cousin. She gets free vacation packages and asked me to be her traveling buddy, and of course I readily agreed. She's easy to talk to and has been a huge support during some difficult times. In the past, Frank was more than cooperative when I wanted to travel without him, but it didn't take me long to understand his generosity. Let's just say he enjoyed his time alone with his addiction and could do whatever he wanted. Over time, I noticed that the hugs and kisses upon my arrival became shorter and less intimate. The next day, my miserable life of being ignored continued, and intimacy in the bedroom was scarce.

But this trip was different. I felt so free because I knew that I'd come home and not have to worry about what he's done. I would not expect any attention, which is fine with me because it was all a show on his part. I had a wonderful time and didn't worry about anything. But the most important thing I realized was that I rarely thought about him and didn't miss him like I used to. Now I'm wondering how long this friend thing is going to last.

Since I've been home, he's once again trying to find a reason to come over every day, but I'm controlling the situation. When he leaves, it feels like he sincerely wants a hug. I oblige, but now I've set a boundary on the kisses—no more on the mouth—which he is complying with. It just feels wrong because a kiss on the lips is very personal and intimate to me. I now realize that the intimacy I once had for him is gone.

He continues to wear his wedding ring and said he feels like I will always be his wife. I told him I didn't think that is healthy thinking. But he still holds on to the idea that we will once again be lovers because God can do miracles, and it appears the man is actually expecting one. Now, because I don't know the mind of God, there is the possibility that it may be His will, but Cat is certainly not interested in going down that road again!

I asked him if he'd really thought about what it would be like if we actually got back together. It could be stressful for him because he'd be walking on eggshells around me and be fearful about making a mistake. But I know for a fact that I'll never trust him again in that area. His reply was that God can do anything, and he's holding on to his faith. I feel so incredibly sorry for him that it makes me want to cry. It's obvious that he's trying so hard to earn my love and trust again, but what he doesn't understand is I haven't had this much peace for over nineteen years. It feels good. I feel like I've been let out of jail, and there's no way I would put myself in that position again.

During that conversation, I told him that maybe someday he would find a woman he was more compatible with, and if he had control of the addiction, it could be a new beginning for him. Maybe *that* was God's plan. I also assured him that I would never sabotage his happiness by telling a woman about our marriage and the ugly past. I truly want him to be happy because I love him as a person. I don't want him to be lonely and feel unloved. I know how that feels, and I wouldn't wish it on anyone. Of course, his response was that he'll never be interested in another woman and has no desire to even date. We'll see.

In Chapter Nine of *Get Off My Porch*, I made commitments for my recovery plan. I'm going to go through each one and see which ones I've now conquered. I believe I've come a long way, but I still struggle with some of them. So, let's see how my report card looks.

PART IV: MY PORCH LIGHT

I'm going back to piano lessons to finish the course because <u>I do play well</u>.

I haven't gone back to my lessons, but I have been taking time each day to sit down for a half hour and practice my most difficult piece ever: "Moonlight Sonata" by Mr. Ludwig van Beethoven. I've now completed four days of my commitment and am having a great time! I'm tripping over the keys somewhat, but I'm able to focus and intend to have it down pat by Christmas.

I'm going to start wearing bright-colored clothes because <u>my body's not so bad</u>.

I've been wearing bright colored clothes more but am still uncomfortable wearing them around Frank because I always felt he was judging me for my imperfections. I've worn them a few times around him, but not much. I know this is all psychological, but I'll get there.

I'll sing when I want to because <u>I have a good voice</u>.

Yes, yes! I'm even singing to commercials, and it's great. My dog Miss Babette seems to like it, too. My dad would be so proud of me because singing was his biggest passion in life. Maybe he's singing with me from Heaven...you never know.

I'll laugh and joke again because <u>I am a happy person</u> by nature.

By golly, I am a happy person these days. Now that I've stepped away from a couple of people who have been emotionally cruel, I have peace of mind because I know they're the ones with a problem. Peace is a beautiful thing!

I'll wear my shorts in the summertime because <u>I have shapely legs</u>.

I'm not doing so well with this one. I've worn them around the house a little bit and have gone out in the backyard only because I have a privacy fence. I did wear them once in public, but I wasn't comfortable. I think it's because I'm still a little self-conscious about my belly.

I'll not compare myself to younger women because <u>I look pretty good for my age</u>.

I'm not comparing myself to anyone now when I'm by myself or with a friend, but I still catch myself occasionally doing it when I'm with Frank in public. It angers me that he still has that type of control over me, but this was one of the most hurtful things I had to deal with. I know it shouldn't matter now, but this is an extremely tough one to get past because I watched him objectify younger women the entire time we were married.

I'll lose fifteen pounds because <u>I want to be healthy</u> (and look better in my clothes).

I'm happy to report that I have lost those fifteen pounds, but I think I probably need to lose five or ten more. I do have to focus on toning up as well. It's amazing what one can do when stress goes away. I feel really good about myself and am proud of myself.

I'll start making jewelry again and doing crafts because <u>I'm very artistic</u>.

I now have a display in a local craft mall of my new design of jewelry. I finally took the plunge, got my beads out, and got to work. It felt good to create something and use my God-given talent again.

I'll read for fun and not education because <u>I enjoy it</u>.

Not only do I read for fun now, but I have been getting up, making coffee, and sitting on my patio almost every morning for sometimes two hours reading my books and listening to my birds. I'm taking this retirement thing very seriously now!

I'll dance in my kitchen if I want to because <u>I like to dance</u>.

PART IV: MY PORCH LIGHT

I'm not doing much of this but would still love to take ballroom dancing lessons. Since I was an aerobics instructor for thirty years, I do have rhythm, so maybe someday I can make that happen.

I'll spend more time with family and friends because <u>I'm a social butterfly</u>.

Oh my goodness—I'm really enjoying myself. My younger sister and I are spending more time together, and I've reconnected with a lot of my friends for "girl days." I have some wonderful people in my life that I've missed so much, and it feels good to be around people that I love and trust.

I'll not let Frank steal my passion for life because God said <u>I don't have to</u>.

I think it's pretty obvious this is not a problem anymore. The addict in him took me down so hard that I'd forgotten what it felt like to have the freedom to be myself and enjoy life. I believe the only reason I've been able to accomplish so many of my goals was because I have gotten so close to God and literally put my life in his hands. My faith is over the top now, and I'll *never* let go of Him.

I believe I'll give myself a B+ right now. I don't mean to sound conceited, but after I read over what I've been typing, I am so very proud of myself and know God's proud of me too!

I bought myself a new devotions book, and I like to look at the scriptures in it. I usually start with my birthday and then my children's birthdays. The one I found pretty much sums up this chapter. It was on my son Jeff's birthday, so I'll close with this:

> *"Blessed is she who has believed that the Lord would fulfill his promises to her."*
>
> —Luke 1:45

Chapter 43

LESSONS LEARNED

I'm beginning to feel like my life has passed by so quickly. There are so many things I would have done differently if I'd known what the outcome would have been, but we can't predict the future. I could "what if" all day long, but it won't change the past.

I haven't written for awhile because I've been dealing with the sadness of how damaged our marriage was. I had to face the reality that I had no choice except divorce because I can't put my health in danger again. Another bout with a compromised immune system could be the death of me, and I'm not willing to take that chance. I may not be so lucky next time. My poor body has taken such a beating. My health has not been totally restored yet, so I have to be proactive at all times and continue to build up my immune system.

I can't say I'm over the sadness yet, but I'm getting better. I had the "poor little ole me" attitude for a while and a few pity parties for myself. Then I got mad all over again because this is so unfair—if he had fixed things a long time ago there wouldn't have been a divorce. All I asked for was to be loved the way a man is supposed to love his wife. Then God came to the rescue (again) and reminded me that I was dealing with an addict.

Even though I use my sense of humor throughout this book, pat myself on the back for the victories, and talk about the strength I've gained through my newfound knowledge, *this has not been easy for me*. I still fall down emotionally but am able to pull myself back up more quickly now. I have good days and bad days, but I know if I'm to live a peaceful and fulfilling life I must stay the course. But above all, I've learned to stand up for myself. I deserve to be happy, and if I have to live alone to have peace of mind, joy, and happiness so be it.

PART IV: MY PORCH LIGHT

In my younger years, I was like most women. I wanted to be married to my knight in shining armor, have children, and live happily ever after with my beloved precious husband through the golden years. Unfortunately, my life didn't work out that way. But, I *was* fruitful and *did* multiply, so it was worth everything I went through to have my sons.

The past twenty years with Frank have been the worst years of my life. Do I resent Frank's emotional abuse? Of course I do! In all honesty, I've not gotten over that yet because I'm too busy trying to put myself back together again. I try to believe I've forgiven him, but I haven't. Even though we get along extremely well for a couple of old divorced people, there are times when my resentment takes over and I have to ask him to leave. I've been totally transparent with him about how PTSD can kick in with no warning, and I have a tremendous education on his addiction. But since we can't feel each other's emotions, sometimes it's difficult to help each other work through a bad situation. But we're learning quickly when to put some space between us.

I know my emotional problems can be permanently fixed with determination and work, but Frank will have to stay vigilant the rest of his life to stay clean. He's being so kind and trying hard to prove that he's worthy of being my friend, but bad memories get in the way sometimes. I know it's all psychological and something I have to conquer regardless of whether the friendship works out or not.

Being married to Frank has been a learning experience to say the least. Last week I had another one of those "aha" moments, and I'm still not sure how I feel about it. I realized that I have no business being married to anyone until I make some serious changes in myself. Of course, *my* plan is to fly solo for the rest of my life, but God may have other plans…we'll see. I discovered that I'm a soft target because I'm a team player and will do anything to get along. I'm easily controlled and manipulated because I'm "such a nice gal." Being kind and giving is a good thing, but I'm learning that I have to be careful around people who'll take advantage of me and set boundaries when necessary.

I'm a good listener and am there for those I love when they have a problem. But during this tough time in my life, I found out that a few of those people could care less about what I'm going through. I now realize that the relationships were pretty much one-sided and not in my favor. I still talk to them sometimes, but I don't make much of an effort to keep in touch.

I've learned so much in the past year that has helped me get to where I am today. The following are the lessons I've learned. It's not been easy and has caused a lot of pain, but I believe I'm becoming a stronger person because I've applied the knowledge I gained through counseling and research.

UNCONDITIONAL LOVE

Not everyone is capable of unconditional love. I was too trusting and assumed if I loved with all my heart that I would receive that same love back. As a child I learned to "do unto others as I would have them do unto me." That's all well and good if everybody follows that rule, but some people don't. I carried that childlike faith into my adult life, got my feelings hurt countless times, and went through extreme emotional pain by staying in crippled relationships waiting for the favor to be returned. But now I know the signs and will sever toxic relationships with no guilt if necessary. I don't want or need that type of love, thank you very much!

PART IV: MY PORCH LIGHT

HATRED

I now realize that I brought this horrible emotion on myself by "staying in the game" and not giving up on the people I loved. I was so naïve! Just because I love someone doesn't mean they're going to treat me well or respect me. I had to admit that there are inconsiderate, selfish, and hateful people in this world. I didn't want to admit I had attached myself to some of those people, but in my defense, they seemed loving and kind to begin with. But I will say this: I loved them the right way, so I have no guilt about how I've treated *them*.

Since toxic individuals usually don't have a conscience, they will go on with their life without any guilt about how they've treated you. I've lost *absolutely nothing* by stepping away from them. But what I've *gained* is peace because they can't hurt me anymore. Yes, it is difficult to sever a relationship and will hurt for awhile, but keep in mind, the hurt they've instilled in you will go on forever if you stay in the relationship. *Temporary pain is much easier to deal with than ongoing pain.*

FEAR

I've heard it said many times that "fear not" is mentioned in the Bible 365 times. That's one for every day of my life! I personally have not taken the time to count them, but from what I understand it's been done and is true. I've experienced so much fear in my adult life—most of it based around men. I've allowed them to bully, control, manipulate, and use me so much that it's embarrassing. But there were times I was truly in physical danger and could have died or been disabled for life.

I believe it's natural to be fearful in certain situations, but my fears with Frank were rejection and abandonment. I've never loved a man the way I loved him, and to be treated like I was nothing became more than I could handle. Instead of remembering my worth as a child of God, I gave him the power to hurt me by giving him control. I can't undo the past, but what I've learned from this hard lesson is that *I can walk away and be happier than I was in the relationship.*

Emotional abuse and intimacy abandonment are terrible things. You can't force an emotional abuser to treat you right, but you can treat *yourself* right by removing yourself from the situation. Was it hard to do? You betcha! But I'm so grateful that God stayed with me and gave me the courage to take my life back again. Now I "fear not"—he's just a mortal man.

SHAME

I was never ashamed of my body before I got involved with Frank. I was disappointed when I was younger because at age twenty I was built like a twelve-year-old boy. No curves, no cleavage, just straight up and down like a ruler. But after I had my first child—boom! Cat was a real live woman! I didn't marry Frank or my other ex-husband because I needed them—I married them because I loved them. I spent over forty years trying to be happily married, so I'm not single again for lack of trying.

When I started dating Frank, I had a nice figure, was considered attractive, and was still getting attention from other men. In fact, I had accepted a date with two different men to go to dinner. Frank and I were friends at the time, and when I told him about the dates, he too asked me out on a date. Of course, knowing him well (I thought) I said yes, broke off the dates with the other men, and the relationship began. He didn't seem to have a problem with my physical appearance until I married him, and then things changed drastically.

My shame came from his lack of attention, pornography, and objectification of women. After several years of his disgusting behavior, when I looked in the mirror I no longer saw myself as pretty or desirable because the man I loved didn't want me. Now, I feel so guilty for judging myself so harshly based on an addict's behavior.

Today, I feel quite shapely and lovely because his opinion doesn't matter anymore. (By the way, I got hit on yesterday in Walmart by a man I used to know, and it felt good! Of course, I'm not interested in a relationship, so I kindly let him know that I'm flying solo these days.) I've learned that my shame was unfounded because he's the one with the problem, and I need to be grateful because God has allowed me to maintain a youthful appearance and my health is getting better all the time. Shame can lead to destructive behavior, and I'll not be ashamed of my body for one more second of one more day!

REJECTION

My mother's rejection forced me to walk away. She's cruel and can't be trusted, and I won't ever put myself in that position again. I used to think it would be a sin to sever a relationship with a family member, but it's not. We're all related in God's eyes, but we're not all compatible. If their behavior is detrimental to your health or happiness, then you may need to move on. People who are unhappy, envious, or jealous can be vindictive. I have an aunt who I loved dearly all my life, but because she jumped in the mud with my mother I had to step away from her as well. Too many people "love the one they're with" with no thought that their wagging tongues and hateful comments about someone they're not in a dispute with will eventually pass through the grapevine.

Frank and his daughter also rejected me. They were both manipulators and controllers, so I didn't have a chance. But I know God will never reject me. Plus, I still have family members and wonderful friends who love me unconditionally.

TRUST

I got a *huge* education on trust. I found out that I was too trusting and assumed I could trust everyone I had a relationship with. But when we told our family and friends about the addiction and initial separation, a couple of family members (not our friends) twisted our words and lied in an attempt to put us both in a bad light. At the time, they seemed sympathetic and understanding. That was when I learned to not listen to their words but watch their behavior. Needless to say, I don't trust these people anymore, and if I'm in a conversation with them, I'm very selective about the topics I talk about. I rarely discuss our situation, and if the topic comes up, I don't give them any ammunition.

SELF-CARE

I've always taken care of my health and been particular about my appearance. But I had to learn to take care of my emotions, which hasn't been easy because of my PTSD. Today has been pretty tough because I had several negative events happen in two days. I figured out that when I'm overwhelmed, that's when I need to turn to God and tell him how grateful I am for all He's done. Two of the problems have been resolved, but the "biggie" is still trying to take me down. So, that's when I decided to write more in this chapter. I discovered that writing calms me down because I have to stay focused. I'm getting much better about dealing with my emotions, but I haven't mastered it yet. But I have to remember that I'm a work in progress. Self-care is critical during recovery.

TIME

I didn't realize how precious time was. I'm not talking about the rat race of "not enough hours in the day." I'm talking about taking time for myself, which is very doable. Not because I'm retired—I'm a *very active* senior citizen! I could easily fill my day with housework, crafts, hanging out with my family and friends, projects around the house, shopping just because I'm bored, helping others, snoozing on the couch, watching television, etc.

I've always enjoyed quiet time and am one of the few people who can go through an entire day without having the television on. When I started dating Frank, whenever he came to my house the first thing he'd do was turn on my television. He just couldn't understand how I could go through my day without "background noise." But now my ability to be in a quiet atmosphere has come in handy. When I get emotionally messy, I'm able to process my thoughts easier and have serious time with God, which always comforts me. I've learned that I can slow down my pace and relax, unless there's a real emergency or something's on fire. Sometimes I spend as much as two hours sitting on the patio, drinking coffee, and reading.

Before the separation, I usually woke up and hit the floor running. I'd clean a house that didn't need to be cleaned and find anything physical to do to avoid dealing with my negative emotions. I'd go to work at the health club exhausted and come home dead tired. I've even done laundry in the middle of the night when I couldn't sleep due to intrusive thoughts. Now *that* should have told me I was an emotional wreck because laundry is one of my least favorite chores.

Most people watch too much television. If you would add up the hours you spend in front of the TV, you'd be amazed at how much time you actually have. People who live alone tend to get lonely, but I don't have that problem. Now that I'm older, I intend to take advantage of my time and enjoy my life. Of course, I watch television at some point each day, but it doesn't control me. Time is a gift, and I'm really learning to appreciate it.

GRATEFULNESS

As we go through life raising our children, working, and combating difficult times, we tend to focus more on the negative instead of the positive. Life becomes much like a hamster wheel that never stops. During all this chaos, we forget to be grateful for the good things because we're too focused on what we consider "survival mode." We talk too much about "getting through the day" and dread the tomorrow that's ahead of us because it too will probably be a challenge.

If people would just stop thinking negatively and look around them, they'd see so many things to be grateful for. I know this because I was so wrapped up in my own misery that I'd forgotten about the many, many blessings God has given me. Once I hit bottom, the only other direction I could go was up, and I'm so glad I had the sense about me to stop and *really* think about what He's done for me. I would not be sitting at my computer right now if He hadn't restored my health. Once I realized that His love is *truly* unconditional, everything changed.

I'm becoming a different person now because I focus more on Him than I do on my problems, and that gives me peace. I do fall down sometimes, but now I pop back up quickly. I've learned that I can't depend on others for my happiness. I choose peace over chaos and God over the people who are so engrossed in their own lives and problems that they have no room for me. I can't say this about all my relationships because I've been blessed with some awesome people and have learned to really appreciate them. So please learn to be grateful even through adversities. You'll be amazed at how calming it can be. I now understand and live with the "peace that passes understanding," and it's beautiful!

VULNERABILITY

This was a biggie for me! To put our story out there was really scary to begin with because I was afraid some people might judge us. They certainly did—but it wasn't the ones we thought it would be. Frank and I got hacked up pretty bad by a few people who we thought would support us and understand. But instead, they made up their own version of our situation, told lies about us, and set out to destroy our reputations. We still don't understand their need to attack, but at this point it doesn't matter because we don't have to deal with them anymore.

On a good note, that's when we were able to separate the goats from the sheep. It wasn't easy to step away from them, but we knew it was necessary. Now, we can relax and depend on the *real and true relationships* we have, and we're both so grateful that they love us unconditionally. Personally, we're glad they showed their true colors because it sure makes our lives easier!

I've learned that being vulnerable isn't a bad thing. People can't help you if they don't know the whole story. No one is clean in this life, and everyone has something ugly in their past because we're all capable of sinning. But the trick is to learn from that sin, repent, and not repeat it. However, there are those who will use that information as a weapon to make themselves look better, and shame on them. If they need to use someone else's pain to build themselves up, they definitely need help too, but pride gets in the way.

I'm not ashamed of what Frank and I have gone through. Any addiction is difficult, and lives can be torn up if the addict doesn't get help. He was struggling with something that changed who he was, which in turn changed who I was. We're both doing our own damage control, but the knowledge we've attained is priceless. I can't speak for him, but going through this terrible ordeal has made me a stronger person and brought me closer to God. I'm very grateful for that.

FAITH

I thought I had real faith before all this happened, but now I realize I didn't. Faith is so powerful when you *really* tap into it. To believe in something you can see is easy, but until you learn to believe in that which is *not* seen you haven't experienced faith at all! The most important thing I did that taught me about true faith was to verbally say "thy will be done" *every day, mean it,* and *believe it.* I end every prayer with "thy will be done." I've given Him complete charge of my life now because I know that I can really trust him. The blessings I'm receiving now are overwhelming, and they just keep coming.

I decided to do some self-marketing to get into the counseling facilities, and I had only sent one email to a popular facility (which I haven't heard back from yet). Then, Frank told me about an excellent counselor he'd heard about and suggested that I send an email to promote my book. *Two days later,* this counselor responded and wants me to speak on her podcast and be on her partner's show. She does training seminars for Partner Trauma as well as couples and family counseling. She hasn't even read my book yet!

My desire is to help partners and eventually be a speaker. When I got her email, I read it probably five or six times and couldn't even speak. I couldn't believe this was happening. This woman is serious and really excited about my book. What in the world is going on here? It's simple…God knew my desire and commitment to help people and opened a door, and Cat is going to run with it full speed ahead! As you've probably gathered by now, I'm not shy. I have some important things to say because I've learned the hard way by falling down, whining, and being a victim until I stood up and said, "That's enough!"

I had an amazing thing happen to me a few weeks ago at a gas station. I was kind of in a melancholy mood that day and was anxious to get home to my sanctuary. I went inside to make a purchase, and the man who waited on me was one of the kindest people I've ever met. After he bagged my merchandise and I told him to have a good day, he said this: "I give you the light you see (he pointed to the light above me), the air you breathe (he circled his arm around) and my smile (it was a beautiful smile)." Needless to say, that man turned my emotions around, and I realized there are a lot of good people out there. I'd like to think he was an angel.

"Faith comes by hearing and hearing by the Word of God."

—Romans 10:17

Chapter 44

I WILL SURVIVE

I'd like to dedicate this chapter to my precious friend Laura. I'm so blessed to have her in my life. I don't believe you meet friends like Laura by accident—I think God selects those who are *worthy* of being her friend. If you put a white robe and halo on Laura, you'd swear she was an angel straight from Heaven. I would trust Laura with absolutely *anything* in my life.

Laura carries herself with dignity and grace. She's the perfect example of a good Godly woman. She loves unconditionally and has integrity. If Laura says she's going to do something, you can bet it will be done. Every time I see Laura, her arms are open for a hug and her smile lights up the room.

I hadn't seen her in a long time because my world was turned upside down and I was dealing with a lot of emotions. Last week I contacted Laura and told her about the addiction and divorce. She was so sympathetic and supportive. She knew we'd been having problems and was sad we didn't make it. We set a time to meet for lunch and were both anxious to get together. The next day, she sent me a text with the link to the song "I Will Survive" by Gloria Gaynor. I laughed my tail off because that had already become "my song." When it comes on the radio, I turn it up and sing at the top of my lungs. Was that a coincidence? I think not.

We went to our favorite Chinese restaurant, and Laura was all ears. She listened to my story while displaying her expertise of using chopsticks, which still amazes me. She sat there calmly, kept eye contact, and patiently listened. I could *feel* the sympathy and love. Then she assured me I was going to be okay because I was a strong woman.

I know I can call Laura anytime—day or night—and she'll be available for me. And, she knows I'll be there for her. Now *that's* what friends do. We're so equally yoked. My friends are a gift, and I'm so fortunate to have so many special people in my life who I can trust to not judge me or ignore my needs. They've all helped me tremendously with my recovery. So I want to thank all my precious friends for being there for me.

When I think of the word "survive," I imagine a situation where there's no money for food, no place to live, or a serious health problem which could result in death. But I've never thought of survival when it comes to emotions. Negative thoughts can lead to anxiety and depression, which can indeed become a serious problem. God wants us to be happy and live a fulfilling life, but when someone you love treats you so badly that you have to break off the relationship, there will be a lot of emotions you'll have to deal with. Casual relationships are much different than loving relationships. When you *really love* someone, there's total trust, but when that trust is broken so is your heart. You don't just throw your hands up and say "all gone." It goes much deeper than that, and it hurts. I'm not just dealing with Frank emotionally but also with my mother.

My conversation with Laura really made me stop and think about my current situation. I'm really not lonely because I have the freedom to go where I want, see my friends, and create a new normal. But there was still something missing, and I finally figured out what it was. God made man and woman to be in an intimate relationship that's pure and loving, and I haven't had that for almost twenty years. I'm not talking about sex—I'm talking about being with someone who loves me unconditionally.

Men are supposed to be our protectors and providers. Frank was a good provider, but he didn't protect the marriage. I've told myself many times that the addiction was the reason he mistreated me, but I'm not willing to use that as an excuse for his behavior anymore. Godly love doesn't work that way. I now believe that he never loved me and I was merely a matter of convenience. He was a good friend but not what I needed in a husband.

Now I'm going to ask God to send me a man who'll love me the way he's supposed to. I'll not marry again, but I'd sure like to have someone who'll make me feel loved and wanted. I want to get out and have some fun and enjoy the rest of my life. I'm ready to be rid of the painful past and move on. I would be willing to commit to a man for the rest of my life if he treats me with the dignity and respect I deserve. But now that I have the freedom to be in control of my own life, marriage scares me. That's pretty sad, but it's easier to step away from a failed relationship than a marriage.

Frank and I are doing well with the friendship, but there's no way in the world I'm going to step back into the intimate part of the relationship again. He still says he's waiting for God to perform a miracle and bring us back together as a loving couple, but what he doesn't understand is I can't emotionally do that again. He says he's ready to love me the way God intended, but it's just too late. I truly feel sorry for him, but I have to do what's right for me now.

I've written about our story for almost a year. It's been very difficult for me at times, but it has definitely helped with my recovery. Thanksgiving has passed and we're headed for Christmas, which is starting to bring back some terrible memories for me because that's when I made the decision to separate and possibly divorce him. The year 2017 was a horrible year for me because that's when he totally pushed me away and accepted the addict as his first love.

I had myself convinced that I'd forgiven him, but I'll admit freely now that I haven't. I've really tried to, but I just can't seem to let go of how he degraded, disrespected, and emotionally abused me. I'm sure God understands that it's going to take some time for me to forgive Frank. It appears that he's doing well in his recovery, but I don't believe I'll ever be able to trust him again in an intimate relationship. However, I do trust him as a friend, and hopefully we can become good buddies again. I don't know what God's plan is for me now as far as relationships go, but my hope is that he'll send me someone to love because I have so much love to give.

  I wish you well and hope you'll be able to survive the pain you've suffered from being involved with a sex addict. I promise that I'll continue to pray for you as well as the addict because they need help as badly as you do. I pray that my books have helped you and that you'll rise above your pain and become the person God intended you to be. The road to recovery will be extremely difficult, but *you can do it* because with God, all things are possible!

Chapter 45

DEAR GOD

Dear God,

I learned about you when I was just a child, but I didn't totally understand what you were all about. I pictured you as a huge and beautiful entity that sat in a humongous chair up in the clouds. When I misbehaved, I imagined you were looking down at me with a frown on your face, but I pictured you smiling at me when I was a good girl.

As I grew up and encountered the usual problems of maturing, I didn't think about you much until I had a problem that was too big for me to handle. During those times, I'd pray and ask you to fix it. Sometimes it took a long time for the problem to be resolved, and I didn't understand why you allowed me to go through the pain. I didn't realize that you were teaching me some very valuable lessons.

When I held my two sons for the first time, I was overwhelmed by the beauty of your creation and felt so close to you. But then I got so busy being a mom and working that once again I put you on the shelf until I needed you. I ran a thousand miles an hour and was in a bad marriage, but I only reached out to you when my tears became uncontrollable.

When I married Frank, I kept you very close because I was so thankful to have a life partner who appeared to be a match made in Heaven. When things started to fall apart, I prayed, but when things didn't get any better, I started wallowing in self-pity. Over time, my prayers became ritualistic with little emotion.

Between Frank's betrayal, my mother's emotional abuse, and my sickness, I began to believe I was being punished for something, but I couldn't figure out what I'd done that warranted such a miserable life.

PART IV: MY PORCH LIGHT

But now I realize I never stopped believing in you—I gave up on myself. Little did I know you were there for me all along, but I stopped reaching out to you and started losing faith in myself. I felt helpless and hopeless.

When I discovered that natural herbs were the solution to my health problems, I was so grateful for the healing plants you created and once again got closer to you. But I still had a miserable marriage and an addict to deal with. I didn't lose faith at that point, but I definitely lost hope.

Last year after Frank went to counseling, I latched on to you, and now I'll never let go. That was the smartest thing I've ever done in my life. I now understand what "peace that passes understanding" means, and it's awesome!

I humbly thank you for never giving up on me even though I'd given up on myself. Now that I understand the power of prayer I will reach out to you instead of trying to handle bad situations myself. I realize there are people who will hurt me, but your love is unconditional. I know that I can let go of those people without guilt because they steal my peace of mind and happiness.

I'm honored that you chose me to write this book. Though it's been difficult for me at times, you've been there to help me stay grounded. I've discovered so much that has helped me with my recovery through the extensive research you encouraged me to do. I now understand that I must share my knowledge in order to help others who are in pain.

Now that I'm in my senior years, I wish I would have stayed closer to you during the difficult times in my life. I know I would have handled things differently and saved myself a lot of grief. I humbly apologize for my ignorance and promise that I'll keep you by my side for the rest of my life.

I want to thank you for all you've done for me, what you're doing for me right now, and what you're going to do for me in the future. The "porch light" in my heart burns bright now because of your Son who gave his life for me.

Finally, I want to thank you for choosing me to be the mother of my precious sons, Jeff and Mark. They will always be my most treasured gift from you, and I love them dearly.

Love, Cat

ABOUT THE AUTHOR

Cat Clark was a nationally certified personal trainer, aerobics instructor, and choreographer. She also worked in the legal field for fifteen years. Today she is a licensed jewelry designer and enjoys a wide variety of crafts. Her life as a retiree is very active with friends, family, and her ever-present beloved dog, *Miss Babette*. She spends time with God and all His creation while feeding birds and squirrels in her mini *Garden of Eden*. She loves playing the piano and is about to complete her final series, at which point she will go on to play the masterpieces. Cat lives in Illinois and has been blessed with two wonderful sons, daughter-in-laws, four granddaughters, and a great-granddaughter.

Made in the USA
Columbia, SC
25 August 2023